Retire Smart

by

David & Virginia Cleary

ALLWORTH PRESS, NEW YORK

For Marguerite and Demetrius

With thanks to the American Medical Association; Brown Shoe Company; Chief Jim Brown; William Brownell; Dr. Robert N. Butler; J.J. Casey; Robert Driver; Florida Hospital/Orlando and Florida Hospital/Waterman; Cynthia Freeman, R.D.; Thomas Hanifen; Lake Sumter Mental Health Center and Hospital; Leesburg Regional Medical Center; Thomas Mullins; National Institute on Aging; and Jack Slater for special help on health and technical matters. (Many other esteemed helpers are mentioned informally by name, here and there, throughout this book. We thank and bless them all.)

Published by Allworth Press, an imprint of Allworth Communications, Inc. 10 East 23rd Street, New York, NY 10010

Distributor to the trade in the United States: Consortium Book Sales & Distribution, Inc. 1045 Westgate Drive, Saint Paul, MN 55114-1065

Book design by Douglas Design Associates, New York

NY.Library of Congress Catalog Card Number: 93-71917

ISBN: 1-880559-09-9

Table of Contents

Part I — Easing into Retirement

Part II — Location and Housing

Part III — Making Your Money Last Longer

Part IV — Helping Yourself to Health

Part IV — Helping Yourself to Health (Continued)

Part V — What Would You Like to Do Today?

Part I

Easing into Retirement

The Best of Both Worlds

Welcome to the time of life where everything comes together.

You've made it through the hassle of the upward-striving years and into the rewarding age of new, first-time freedoms. New freedom from alarm clocks and time clocks. First-time freedom to live almost anywhere. Freedom to do more of what you want to do and less of what you have to do. And above all, freedom to spend more time becoming the person you've always wanted to be.

Now begins your double life, the age of being important and needed — in both the world of work and the world of leisure.

You picked a good time. Never has the outlook for retirees been so inviting. Breakthroughs in medicine, and an explosion in wellness programs, have added quality years to your life. Plus, a revolution in life-styles offers you a whole new choice of stimulating activities to make each day more important.

You Are Needed

With all your new freedom, you won't be withdrawing from old friends who are still punching the clock. The world of work, with all its problems, still needs your experience and your insights, as either a volunteer or a paid part-timer. And now you can lend a helping hand in the best possible way: on a pick-and-choose basis, where and when your guidance is asked for ... and will be appreciated.

There will be times when you can be highly supportive by just being there, being available as an understanding listener.

How We Can Help

To keep up with the doubling demands on your time, you will need, of course, to be more and more selective. This compact-but-complete guidebook can help you do it in two ways: It can steer you more swiftly and surely into a more stimulating and fulfilling — and healthy — life-style.

And it can save you from repeating many of the time-wasting and often costly mistakes the rest of us have made.

Perhaps most important of all, it can alert you early to some of the inevitable problems all retirees face — and show you how to handle them.

Beware Euphoria

Your dictionary makes it sound harmless: "eu-pho-ria — an often unaccountable feeling of well-being or elation." Euphoria, often closely linked with retirement, is a happy feeling that can hurt you. Take a moment to read what it has done to some of our friends. The stories are all true.

George and Anna T. headed south from Pittsburgh with a long-cherished dream of a swimming pool just outside the back door — and they found it within a week. Their gratitude to their new real estate benefactor bubbled over throughout the closing. A few months later, the county government exercised its right to run a new road through George and Anna's front yard, cutting down four stately oaks in the process. In their euphoric haste, and their euphoric trust in the real estate person, George and Anna had felt there was no need to retain an attorney. An attorney, of course, would have warned them that the survey of their property included an easement for a possible future road.

Look — Don't Leap

Jack and Sue M. went to a real estate seminar during a Chicago blizzard and fell in love with the waterfront haven they saw in glowing color on the screen. They took immediate advantage of a discounted trip south to see the property, agreed it was everything the sales people had claimed, and signed a contract. Later, they had to conclude that the summer heat was more than they ever would be able to adjust to.

Frank and Betty R. collected enough cash at retirement time, in Westchester County, New York, to feel "filthy rich"—but they also had a deep fear of inflation. The solution, a seller of securities assured them, was a portfolio of strong growth stocks. In their euphoric hurry to get on with their retirement, Frank and Betty made a bold purchase and invited the seller to stay for a few drinks. During the next three years, Frank and Betty watched more than half their savings disappear in an ailing stock market.

Read the Fine Print

Bob D., who had always wanted to break away from an Indiana factory and be his own boss, heard of a franchise opportunity that sounded unbeatable — it would even be something in which Fran would like to participate. Now, as a retiree, he was suddenly free to make the *big* move he had always been too timid to make. The prospects were so good that he didn't hesitate to put up his insurance policies as collateral on the bank loan. Within a few months, Bob was complaining to his friends that the franchisor's promises of generous promotional support had all been "just so much hot air." Within a year, the bank foreclosed on the property and kept the insurance policies.

Charlie and Edna K. were golfers who never had had enough time to play. Retirement offered a whole new life style: a brand-new, bargain-priced, manufactured home on the edge of a fairway. They even negotiated an "unbelievable deal" on the home because they had cash in hand. Some months later, they heard disturbing rumors that the owner of their park was in financial trouble. Charlie and Edna, in a sudden panic, put their golf clubs aside and began scrutinizing all their real estate papers. The rumors turned out to be true: the park owner had not given them the promised deed to their property. Charlie and Edna now had more than $60,000 invested in a home with no proof of ownership. It could not be sold.

These stories are all true, with no trace of exaggeration, and we could tell you many more. The names have been changed, of course, to spare our friends any further embarrassment.

Proceed with Caution

The dictionary described euphoria as an "often unaccountable feeling." In the case of the retiree, it is seldom *"unaccountable."* It springs from a sudden, rushing feeling of total, carefree *freedom*. Freedom to launch an *instant* new life with no restraints.

It's a common feeling. We know; we were one of the couples you just read about. We and many others learned the hard way that, in the euphoria that comes with retirement, it's wise to make haste at about half our normal speed.

Who Invented "Retirement"?

*I*t was *not* America's FDR.

In 1881, the year before Franklin Delano Roosevelt was born, Germany's imperial chancellor, Prince Otto von Bismarck, became the first statesman in Europe to announce a comprehensive plan for social security, offering workers subsidized insurance against sickness, accident, and old age. This "Bismarckian Socialism" would become a model for other countries in Europe.

Bismarck has been described by historians as "a man of violent temperament and ruthless methods who spent his life thwarting the democratic wishes of the German people." So why would he become the father of social security? He had both a minor and a major reason. The minor reason was his belief, as "an extreme conservative," that the state should be paternalistic. The major reason was a conviction that his program would help destroy his main political enemy, the Social Democrats (followers of Karl Marx), by showing them that they could be helped more by their government than by their political party. By 1890, he conceded that his strategy had failed; the Social Democrats had continued to gain in numbers and power.

Why Age 65?

As part of his grand plan, Bismarck picked the age at which he thought workers should retire: 65. It was a purely arbitrary figure and he never applied it to himself. He continued to be a truculent officeholder until the eve of his 75th birthday, when he was summarily fired by Emperor William II for being just too disagreeable to deal with.

(Emperor William II, incidentally, may have picked up some of Bismarck's abrasive management style. The emperor, once a kindly man, became better known to the world later as the German Kaiser Wilhelm of World War I.)

Franklin Delano Roosevelt, like Prince Otto von Bismarck, was the son of a wealthy landowner and moved early into a career of public service. The two men had nothing else in common.

By age 28, three years out of Columbia University Law School, young FDR began the first of two terms as a New York state senator. By age 31, he had been appointed Assistant Secretary of the Navy. In 1920, when he was 38, the Democratic Party nominated him for vice-president of the United States as the running mate of James M. Cox. The Cox-Roosevelt ticket was beaten by Warren G. Harding and Calvin Coolidge — and then, during the following summer, FDR's world collapsed. Polio struck suddenly, paralyzing his legs and dooming him to a wheel chair for the rest of his life.

FDR's Early Retirement

Invalidism was so demoralizing that FDR, at 39, announced his retirement from public life. He would busy himself instead with some old hobbies, like the building of ship models.

But he had a wife of 16 years named Eleanor who refused to let him have his way. It was Eleanor, an indefatigable leader of social causes, who kept him involved in the working world.

In 1928, when he was 46, FDR's supporters asked him to run for the governorship of New York. The man in the wheel chair protested that he needed two more years of treatment to regain his health — but he ran. And he won. And he was reelected two years later with a reputation as a champion of advanced social legislation, including an old-age pension law.

Why Social Security?

In 1932, when he was 50 and still in a wheel chair, the people chose FDR to lead them out of the worst economic depression in U.S. history. Part of his recovery plan was a social security program with a two-fold objective: it not only would protect retirees against undue hardship but would give them an incentive to move out of the work force and make way for younger workers who needed jobs. The Social Security Act ran into a 14-month fight in Congress, but won out and was signed into law on August 14, 1935.

FDR's first-term progress won him a second term in 1936. Then the nation's principal concern changed from jobs to a second World War and

a worn and weary FDR was pressed into an unprecedented third term
— and later a fourth.

When time stopped for Franklin Delano Roosevelt, on April 12,
1945, as he sat in his old wooden wheel chair in his simple cottage in
Warm Springs, Georgia, he was just a little over two months into his 64th
year. He didn't make it to 65.

4

The Resources Around You

*T*here's no need, these days, for any retiree to feel left out and alone. Beyond the close-in support of our family and friends, we seniors are being surrounded by additional circles of support at all levels of government and throughout an increasingly-caring private sector. Here is a handy directory of resources to keep for continuing reference and to share with your friends.

Local Government

Dial 911, the universal, emergency phone number, to report any police, fire, or medical emergency. Your call will be routed automatically to a central answering point. There is no direct charge to you for your call; the cost of 911 service is spread over all phone customers. *Special guidelines*: 1) In *non*-emergency situations, just dial your local police, fire, and medical numbers directly; do not use 911. 2) Do *not* use a *cordless* phone to dial 911 — it can cause false alarms with its pulse signals. 3) If you are choking when you dial 911, or unable to speak for any other reason, your address and phone number will be displayed automatically at the emergency answering point and an operator will call you back for verification. If you cannot speak, the police will be sent to investigate. 4) If you dial 911 accidentally, do not hang up. Instead, just tell the operator you made a mistake — otherwise, the police will be sent to investigate. 5) Please do not dial 911 except in true emergencies involving serious threats to health, safety, or property. Never use the 911 system to report such minor problems as leaky plumbing, animal pests, or a need for highway directions — the 911 emergency system is badly burdened with such nuisance calls.

Community Center. Visit the place and see what they do there.

15

Consumer Information. Your county or city can give you the names and phone numbers for such services as:

- Area Agency on Aging
- Community Care for the Elderly
- Home Health Services
- Home Delivered Meal Program
- Hospitals
- Lawyer Referral Service
- Physicians Referral Service
- Senior Center(s)
- Senior Helpline
- Senior Services.

Cooperative Extension Service. This national, county-by-county service, affiliated with the U.S. Department of Agriculture and with state universities, offers free guidance on home economics and agricultural subjects. The home economics office offers information and guidance on such subjects as nutrition, clothing and textiles, money management, energy conservation, and housing and equipment. The agriculture office offers information and guidance on such subjects as the care of trees, shrubs, and lawns.

Public Health Department. Services vary from area to area, but your public health department usually offers such retiree helps as flu shots and blood pressure screening on a sliding scale of charges. It's worth visiting your local health department to be aware of how they serve the community.

Libraries. The American Library Association urges all retirees to visit their nearest library and examine the various kinds of reference works available there to meet special needs. Large type, for example, may be important to you. Reference works of special appeal to retirees include cook books, computer manuals, bird watchers' guides, quotation books, and historical information of all kinds. Remember, too, that you are entitled to use the Law Library at your county courthouse. A librarian usually will be on hand to help you look up whatever legal information you need.

Public Housing. Most counties and cities have a housing authority or comparable office that offers rental assistance, under a federal grant program, to tenants who need to spend more than 50 percent of their income for housing. Funds are usually limited.

Recreation and Parks Department. Find out what's available in your area: swimming, tennis, golf, shuffleboard, lawn bowling, and other sports.

Schools. Ask about your local adult education courses. Also ask about the wide variety of courses at your nearest community college and your nearest vocational/technical center. The practical knowledge is valuable and the life enrichment can be priceless. Continuing education is also a pleasant way to meet new friends who share your interests.

Senior Center. Visit the place and see what they do there. The typical senior center offers a broad and busy schedule of social, crafts, and physical fitness activities for retirees of all ages. Also, the senior center usually offers day care service as at least a partial alternative to nursing home care.

Sheriff's Department. In some communities, the Sheriff's Department has a "Senior Care Watch," or its equivalent, under which a senior citizen is expected to call the department by a certain time each day. If the call is not received, a deputy will call the senior. If there is no answer, a deputy will be sent to the senior's home to investigate. Ask your Sheriff's Department about this type of service. Note: in some cities, the department of public safety or the fire department rescue group offer a similar "security call" service. Ask the city manager's office about it.

Social Services. Most counties and cities offer an information and referral service to people who have no outside income and need helpful guidance.

Veterans Services. Most counties have an office of veterans services — not an official part of the U.S. Veterans Administration — to help local veterans with their questions about pensions and health care.

Local Private Sector

Chamber of Commerce. Call or visit there for general information about who does what among the local businesses. The Chamber of Commerce cannot, of course, recommend one firm over another, but will be glad to help you with your special questions.

Churches and synagogues. Your local Yellow Pages carry a complete list of places of worship in your area. The broad and varied choice is usually very impressive.

Clubs. Bridge, boating, garden, women's — they're all in the Yellow Pages and they all have some new friends you haven't met.

Doctors. To find a doctor in a new locality, just call the county medical society or any hospital.

Fraternal organizations. See the Yellow Pages. Many of the members of those organizations never joined any group until retirement, so you won't feel like a stranger.

Health maintenance. Every modern hospital offers screening programs for early detection of health problems, and wellness programs to keep you fit. Ask about them.

Mental Health Center. Mental health counseling can help retirees with such common problems as:

- anger management
- anxiety and depression
- chemical dependency
- co-dependency
- eating disorders
- grief
- marital conflicts
- misuse of medications
- psychiatric symptoms
- self-esteem problems
- stress management, and other mental menaces.

Many mental health centers have adult day care programs for older people who are able to lead a generally independent life but need some assistance during the day. Leading mental health centers also offer geriatric residential and treatment services. Fees at mental health centers are based on your income and responsibilities; they can be covered by Medicare and other insurance.

Newspapers. In many areas, local newspapers offer continuous, computerized voice information service to people with Touch Tone phones. Subjects range from business news to sports scores to weather.

Television stations. Most major stations assign a reporter to help viewers who have problems involving consumer fraud and other deceptive marketing practices. Exposing the cheats on TV usually brings faster action than taking the cases to court, and at no charge to the victims.

United Way. Ever since 1887, when two Denver ministers, a priest, and a rabbi launched the first total-community fundraising drive for local health and welfare agencies, United Way has symbolized efficient, voluntary service to the entire local community. United Way now comprises more than 2,000 local United Way organizations, all of them autonomous, under a national banner. Your local United Way serves as a mechanism for raising funds for private sector services, and it also functions as an information and referral center. Services of special interest to retirees include:

- Aging and Adult Services
- Arthritis Foundation
- Better Hearing Institute
- Blind Services
- Congregate Meal Programs
- Consumer Education Services
- Council on Aging
- Diabetes Association
- Food Stamps
- Fraud Hotline
- Geriatric Residential Treatment
- Hearing and Speech Clinic
- Heart Association
- Housing
- Large print materials
- Long-term Care Ombudsman
- Lung Association
- Medical Referral Service
- Medical Transportation
- Nutritional Center for Seniors
- Respite Care
- Senior Counseling Center
- Speech and Language Center
- Visually Impaired Center
- Widowed Persons Service.

Note: the line-up of United Way agencies varies somewhat from place to place, so check with your local United Way about specific services.

Self-Help Support Groups

Support groups, as a helping and healing force, do not compete with physicians, psychiatrists, or other professionals, but occupy a niche all their own. Support groups are usually organized by individuals who have had personal experience with some particular problem and would like to help themselves and others with the same problem by sharing their experience and knowledge. Support groups offer a unique mix of under-standing, insights, and mutual encouragement because the shearer "have all been there."

There are now some half-million different, local support groups in the U.S., concerned with almost every human problem. The exact num-ber is unknown because, as one authority explains, "Any two people who share a problem can start a support group."

Some groups are affiliated with national organizations; some are strictly "local." There are three general types of support groups: 1) Those concerned with addictions, such as Alcoholics Anonymous and Overeaters Anonymous; 2) those concerned with the self-care of such physical and mental illnesses as Parkinson's and Alzheimer's Disease; and 3) advocacy groups for the elderly and other minorities, such as Gray Panthers and Alliance for the Mentally Ill.

Local hospitals, your mental health center, and your United Way can brief you on the various support groups in your area. Here are some typical examples of support groups of special interest to retirees:

- Alcoholics Anonymous and Al-Anon
- Alliance for the Mentally Ill
- Alzheimer's Support Group
- Arthritis Interest Group
- Better Breathers Support Group
- Diabetes Support Group
- Impotency Support Group
- Laryngectomy Support Group
- Ostomy Group
- Overeaters Anonymous
- Parkinson's Support Group
- Stroke Club

Support groups usually welcome all persons who share a particular problem, and they try to raise only enough money to pay their modest expenses. Some of the groups are sponsored in whole or part by hospitals and mental health centers.

State Government

Because retiree services at the state level vary so much from state to state, we suggest you phone — or better yet, stop in personally — and ask your local elected representative in your state legislature about the services your state offers to seniors. Most states offer services like the following, and most of them have toll-free 800 phone numbers:

- Blind Services
- Consumer Protection Hotline
- Health Care Cost Containment Board
    (concerned with physicians, charges)
- Human Rights Advocacy Center
    (concerned with the rights of patients in nursing homes)
- Insurance Customers' Hotline
- Public Service Commission (concerned with rates charged by utilities)

Federal Government

Action, the National Volunteer Agency. This government office funds four programs of interest to seniors, the most important of which is RSVP, the Retired Senior Volunteer Program, now operating through more than 50,000 local organizations with some half-million retired volunteers. RSVP activities range from schools and libraries to the criminal justice system to food banks and crisis hotlines. For local information about RSVP, call your Senior Center or United Way. The other three Action programs for seniors are: VISTA (Volunteers in Service to America), the domestic Peace Corps; Foster Grandparents Program; and Senior Companion Program — all of which vary in size from area to area. For more information, write: Action, the National Volunteer Agency, Washington, DC 20525.

Area Agency on Aging. This national information and referral service, funded by the federal government, offers a wide range of information covering health and safety, housing, crime, and other senior citizen concerns. To get in touch with your state's Area Agency on Aging, call the federal Eldercare Locator (now see Eldercare Locator for additional information).

Consumer Information Center. This publications office offers more than 200 booklets on cars, education and employment, exercise and weight control, health, housing, money management, travel and hobbies, and many other subjects. The center works with more than 40 federal agencies and subagencies to obtain the booklets for distribution, either free or at a modest charge. Mail your request for a free catalog to: Consumer Information Center-2A, P.O. Box 100, Pueblo, Colorado 81002.

Conservation and Renewable Energy Inquiry & Referral Service. This office of the U.S. Energy Department offers free information about caulking, weather stripping, solar energy, recycling, and other energy subjects. Call 1-800-523-2929 (toll free).

Eldercare Locator. This national service, mentioned above in connection with the Area Agency on Aging, gives you easy access to an extensive network of organizations serving older people at state and local community levels throughout the U.S. To get information for yourself — or for any older relative or friend — just call 1-800-677-1116 (toll free). Call between 9 a.m. and 5 p.m., Eastern Standard Time, and have this information ready when you call: 1) The name and address of the older person you are assisting, including that person's ZIP code. 2) A brief, general description of the problem or type of assistance you need. The Eldercare Locator can connect you with information sources for a full range of senior services by giving you the phone numbers of the state or local agencies you need to reach.

Health and Human Services Department. This office offers free booklets explaining Social Security, Medicare, and Food Stamps. Call 1-800-772-1213 (toll free).

Internal Revenue Service. The IRS maintains a variety of free services using toll-free 800 numbers. For a free copy of *A Guide to Free Tax Services* (publication number 910), call 1-800-TAX FORM. For general tax assistance, call 1-800-829-1040. For tax assistance for deaf persons using TDD equipment, call 1-800-829-4059.

Meals on Wheels and Congregate Meal Service. Call your local Senior Services Office or Senior Center. Free lunches for seniors have been offered, under the Older Americans Act, since 1965. Donations are accepted, but not required.

The National Institute on Aging offers a free "Resource Directory for Older People." The book covers national organizations in the field of aging, complete with their names, addresses, and telephone numbers (toll free whenever possible). The list includes Federal Government agencies, professional societies, private groups, and voluntary programs. For your free copy, call 1-800-222-2225 (toll free), or write: Public Information Office, Building 31, Room 5C27, Bethesda, MD 20892.

Peace Corps. This agency, formed in 1961, invites inquiries from seniors who would like to serve as volunteers in developing countries — in Latin America, the Caribbean, Africa, Asia, and the Pacific. The Peace Corps has a special need for retirees with experience in agriculture, forestry and fisheries, education, community development, home economics and nutrition, engineering, math and science, and in many of the skilled trades, from carpentry to welding. For information, call 1-800-424-8580 (toll free). The Peace Corps offers its volunteers a monthly living allowance, health care, language training, support systems, and other benefits.

National Private Sector

AARP— American Association of Retired Persons. This national association was established in 1958 by a retired school teacher, Dr. Ethel Percy Andrus, for the purpose of "bettering the lives of older Americans through service, advocacy, education, and volunteer efforts." It is a nonprofit, nonpartisan organization with more than 33 million members age 50 and over. AARP represents senior citizens at all legislative levels, publishes a magazine and news bulletin, and operates insurance, investment, and pharmacy services. AARP maintains a national headquarters at 1909 K Street, NW, Washington, DC 20049, and a membership processing center at 3200 E. Carson Street, Lakewood, California 90712. Membership dues were set, in 1992, at $8 per year, or $20 for three years, or $45 for 10 years. Anyone age 50 or over can join AARP by sending membership dues to the Lakewood, California office.

Alzheimer's Association, 919 North Michigan Avenue, Chicago, Illinois 60611-1676. This association is an excellent source of information and guidance on Alzheimer's Disease and related disorders.

Ask-A-Nurse. This national information service, which offers answers over the phone to whatever health question you care to ask, is sponsored locally by leading hospitals, whose professionals take turns on the phones. Ask your hospital about this service.

Cancer Information Service. This national resource is sponsored by the American Cancer Society. Call 1-800-227-2345 (toll free) or write to American Cancer Society, Cancer Information Center, 1599 Clifton Road, NE, Atlanta, Georgia 30329.

National Eye Care Project. This national referral service, sponsored by the American Academy of Opthalmologists, enables seniors over 65 to visit an opthalmologist, free. People older than 65 make up half of the blind population of the U.S., and often have limited medical insurance. To qualify for a referral to a volunteer opthalmologist, a person must be a U.S. citizen or legal resident, age 65 or older, and must not have had previous access to an opthalmologist. There are no financial qualifications. Each volunteer opthalmologist will bill the patient's Medicare or other insurance. The costs of eyeglasses, contact lenses, drugs, and hospital services are not covered by the NECP. To get your referral, call NECP, toll-free, at 1-800-222-EYES.

Part II

Location and Housing

"Where Should We Retire?"

*C*lose friends of ours, in recent years, have tried just about all the combinations of where to settle in retirement.

When we first met Kirt Swanes in Jakarta, he was nearing the end of an international banking career and had lived in 14 major countries in Europe, South America, and Asia. We had just arrived in Indonesia as retiree volunteers in the International Executive Service Corps. Kirt intrigued us with his sensitive understanding of these gentle, almost-mystical people who comprised more than 360 ethnic groups and 250 languages, and whose first ancestor had lived more than 100 centuries ago.

"One of these years," we told Kirt, "you're going to have to make a decision about hanging up your track shoes. By now, you've seen it all — the geography and the people — so you must have picked the world's best place for retirement."

Three Criteria

His answer came slowly. "I love the Indonesians and this picture-book land; but I also have a great fondness for Portugal and Ecuador, and a few others. I like friendly people and a mild climate, with lots of spectacular scenery, unique arts, and good fishing. It's hard to pick just one best place.

"I finally picked three criteria," Kirt said, "for comparing all the countries I've seen.

"The least important of the three is climate. In an air-conditioned world, lots of places can qualify on climate,

"The middle requirement is economical living — and that never stays the same anywhere. In this computer age, the bargain places are all reported too fast, get too much hype from the travel writers, and soon are getting crowded. What you heard a few years ago about an area's living costs might not be true today.

26

"That brings me to my number one, most exacting requirement — political stability. No worries ever about property being confiscated. No limitations ever about coming and going. Freedom of speech and everything else." He stopped for a long pause.

"So," we prompted, "where will it be?"

"Back where I came from," he said. "The States. The land of the free. I'll go back where I grew up, in western Washington. Sally and I think it's great family country, with some fishing, rock hunting, and mountaineering that are hard to match."

Close to Home

Meanwhile, back in America, Robert and Patricia Berlin Mitchell were retiring in Glen Rock, New Jersey, and staying right where they were. The only change: no more commuting by car to New York City. He had retired as editor of a business magazine; she had retired as the interior designer at a major university. Along with their career work, they had both been widowed, had put two households together, and now the sons and daughters were all grown and married. "Glen Rock is handy," they said, "for all our kids and their families. They like to come back for get-togethers, and it's nice to have the extra room when they come. We also like being this close to all the attractions of New York City. We might or might not move later to a smaller place."

Walter and Lurabel Colburn decided, after Walter retired from a bone-crunching career coaching football and all other sports, to treat themselves to a second place in the sunbelt. Their home at Lake Chautauqua, near Jamestown, New York, was a summer sports wonderland; but some of the winters could be formidable. They looked in a southern area where they had once vacationed and ordered a new manufactured home that met all their requirements in a prudent, non-extravagant way.

Cliff and Donita Paine, in western Michigan, had co-published a unique hometown newspaper, The Fennville Herald; he had served long years on the school board; and they had raised a family. Then some heart scares persuaded Cliff that it was time for a change in lifestyle. The Paines opted for a new retirement community in nearby Holland. It offered a variety of activities and amenities, including an Adult Congregate Living Facility (ACLF) for the assisted living that might in time be needed. Above all, it was close to family and friends. "We like the four-season Michigan climate," Donita told us, "and our roots are here." How "typical" were all those retiree moves?

Looking Ahead

As we near the Year 2000, the location and housing choices for retirees have formed a definite, predictable pattern. The National Association of Home Builders concluded, in 1992, that most retirees wanted to "do their aging in place." A 1991 survey by The Roper Organization found that the top three reasons why Americans liked their present location were "Like my friends here"... "Family lives close by" ... and "Like the kind of people here." Their feelings about housing and climate were lower on the list.

Most retirees, of course, have ample free time for travel elsewhere when they want a change in climate and scenery.

The home builders also noticed this significant pattern: of the retirees who moved away from their old homes, some 80 percent were moving a distance of less than 200 miles. As a result, specialized retirement communities were appearing near major population centers everywhere, not just in the sunbelt. Inevitably, in this age of acronyms, the now-generation retirement communities have become NORCS — "naturally occurring retirement communities." Del Webb's pioneer Sun City of 1960 in Arizona has now evolved into "active adult communities" in such northern and western cities as Chicago and Dallas. The developers are phasing out the original word *retirement*. They prefer instead to talk about *lifestyles*.

"Retirees no longer move anywhere just to do their aging in idleness," the builders say. "They want to start a whole new lifestyle with kindred spirits of their own age. Retirement, for them, is not just an ending — it's a beginning."

Location Basics

Our friends urge you: in any new, unfamiliar location, try to rent — don't buy — until you have experienced a full year of the local weather. Many retirees who made winter purchases in the balmy south — or summer purchases in the cool north — have since retreated toward happier-medium locations. And if you are moving to another state, you'll be wise to check out its income and other tax rates.

Also, in any location, check the distances from there to the shopping and entertainment places, the health care centers, the airports, and other points of interest to you.

Finally, take time to meet and talk with the people who will become your neighbors. Will they be a congenial group to be with, day after day after day?

For more about the choices in locations, ask your book seller and your librarian about some interesting new books that have arrived recently — but remember that any facts about prices may have changed since the publication date.

Now, for more about the choices in housing — single-family homes, condominiums, manufactured homes, Adult Congregate Living Facilities, and RV living — read on...

Single-Family Homes

Most of us grew up in traditional, single-family homes and we liked the privacy of it. If we owned the place, we also liked the independent feeling that comes with being able to change it any way we pleased. But retirement brings new and different needs.

Now we need to downsize, for easier upkeep or because the kids are grown and away. Or we need a less expensive neighborhood, not as close to the old work area. Or, for health or other reasons, we need or want a gentler climate.

Should We Build Or Buy?

Paul and Jean Ward once built what was to be their ultimate dream home, in the Front Range west of Denver, and they did it with their own hands. They don't like to remember how many nights, weekends, and vacation periods it took. "Never again," they said later. "But at least we learned how a home should be built."

When the time came to build their retirement version of a dream home, they followed this procedure: Find out who the area's most respected builders are, and meet them personally. Decide which ones are most interested in building your particular kind of house. Get their references from both customers and suppliers, and talk with some of the customers. With the customers' permission, check the quality of the "finish work"—moulding joints, caulk seams, and grout lines. Then choose three or more builders as qualified prospects, give them complete specifications, and invite bids.

Retiree Specifications

Retirees who look ahead plan carefully for easier living everywhere in the home, beginning with fewer stairs to climb, and less ladder work in maintaining the place. So the Wards decided on a one-story house with a hip roof (no gable ends to paint on ladders), and aluminum soffit and fascia. Looking ahead, they also specified 36"-wide doorways (wheelchair width), single-lever faucets and door levers instead of knobs (which can be hard to turn if you have a touch of arthritis), and cabinets at heights that do not require awkward reaching or squatting.

Further to minimize painting, they had a choice of aluminum or vinyl siding, or of mixing color with stucco for lifetime color. (They chose the colored stucco.) Inside the home, they reduced housework by putting ceramic tile on their floors, and smooth, synthetic, no-mildew marble in their bathrooms.

They planned extra-spacious bathrooms because privacy, in retirement, is more important than ever before, and bathrooms are the most private places in a home.

Is It Energy Efficient?

With an eye on future electric bills, the Wards had called for the latest booklets of the U.S. Energy Department (just call 1-800-523-2929, toll free), and had arranged with their power company to equip the home with demand meters in order to channel more power to off-peak hours. They also included energy conservation in their landscape planning because proper shading of windows and walls, for example, can reduce air-conditioning energy use by 40 percent or more.

When the bids from the builders were all in, the Wards chose, not the builder with the lowest bid, but the builder who had made the best suggestions for enhancing their plans.

During the construction phase, they could have hired an independent building inspector to check the quality of the work, once after the framing was completed, and then when the house was completed; but they felt qualified to do that for themselves.

Buying an Existing Home

Frederick and Bernice Powers of California, with their six young ones all grown and away, sold their home in Campbell after retirement and moved to a smaller one in Orangevale.

Normally, in buying an existing home, it's wise to pay the modest cost of a professional appraiser who can warn you of any hidden defects in the roof, foundation, and walls; and in the electrical, plumbing, and heating/cooling systems. Lending institutions require such appraisals in order to determine the market value of a home before they make mortgage loans; but a buyer can often improve his bargaining position by arranging for his own appraisal. Mr. Powers, as a professional in the building trades, was able to do his own appraising.

Renewing Older Homes

One or two coats of quality paint can make most existing homes look almost like new again — and most people are pleasantly surprised by the easier application and longer life of today's paints and other coatings. Equally impressive advances await you at the wall coverings, floor coverings, and lighting stores. To blend it all together in a tasteful and imaginative way, consider indulging yourself — perhaps for the first time ever — in the services of a professional interior decorator or designer. Many retail stores offer this service at no charge.

You may also decide to do some remodeling of the bathroom, kitchen, or garage — all of which will add to the resale value, as well as the livability, of your home.

HUD Properties

Bargain hunters will take time to inquire about the continuously-changing selection of homes being offered by the U.S. Department of Housing and Urban Development (HUD). The properties, from single-family homes to condominiums, are all foreclosed properties covered by Federal Housing Administration (FHA) insurance. For a free booklet about HUD properties and how to inspect the ones in your area, call HUD, toll-free, at 1-800-767-4483.

HUD properties usually are available in three categories: renovated, partially renovated, and "as is." To keep its inventory moving, HUD reappraises it every 30 days and makes whatever price cuts are needed. Prospective buyers, after reviewing the HUD prices, can submit lower bids if they wish. HUD wants to sell its properties to owner-occupants, with a low down payment, but will also sell to investors with a much higher down payment.

Along with the federal government's HUD homes, the Veterans Administration offers foreclosures it has acquired under the VA home guarantee program.

Real Estate Agents

The simplest, least expensive way to buy a home is to buy direct from the owner. Your mortgage lender, or an independent appraiser, can help you determine the fair market price.

But very few of the homes on the market have "For Sale" signs, so you probably will need a real estate agent to show you what's available and give you full details.

Real estate agents function both in the selling and the buying of homes. The agent usually collects his commission from the seller — and commissions, under the Federal Anti-trust Law, cannot be fixed; they can vary from area to area.

When a seller puts his home up for sale, he lists it with a real estate agent with a short- or long-term "exclusive" agreement, and usually asks for it to be put into the local multiple listing service (MLS) to make it available to nearly all agents. When the sale is made, the agent who had the first listing will collect a share of the total commission.

Home buyers are advised to talk with two or more agents about their needs, and then to select the agent who seems most knowledgeable, offers the widest selection, and is not favoring any of his own listings. It also is strongly recommended that buyers retain a local real estate attorney to review the sales contract and other relevant documents before any papers are signed.

Condominium Homes

CON-DO-MIN-I-UM. Centuries before it became an American household word, the pompous old Latin word had been the lofty, official government term for joint sovereignty by two nations over a smaller one. Then somebody, in the days of the Roman Empire, applied the concept to housing, and the idea began to spread through Europe. Next, we jump to America, where Florida, in 1963, passed a law authorizing the formation of condominiums.

In housing, the word *condominium* means a system of ownership (not a kind of structure) in which an individual owns one unit in a multi-unit community and has joint ownership of the commonly-owned property.

When the condominium concept came to America, it was hailed by sociologists and economists — not just by builders — as "the wave of the future." The "condo" was an all-in-one answer to the need for mass housing at affordable prices, and to an aspiring public's yearning for such luxurious amenities as game rooms and swimming pools. The condominium, first as an apartment complex, later as an extensive community, introduced a new age of *sharing the good life.*

Ownership Problems

Amidst all the early-year enthusiasm, one giant point was accepted without much questioning: the long-term *ownership* of the condominium would be transferred gradually from the original developer to an elected association of apartment owners—some of whom were rank amateurs at property management, and some of whom were concerned only with protecting their own personal, short-term interests, such as the absentee ownership of rental units.

As a grim consequence, some condominium developers — and condominium associations — ignored the need for prudent maintenance reserves in order to promote their offers of low monthly maintenance charges. Inevitably, in the 1990s, the occupants of those earlier, shortsighted complexes were being shocked by special assessments for major roof, plumbing, and fire safety repairs. In one popular retirement area, an estimated 90 percent of all the local condominium associations had failed to put any funds aside for repairs, even despite the existence of a state law requiring such funds.

Check the Records

It's wise, when shopping for a condominium home, to visit and compare at least three communities, and then to inquire about their reputations at the local Chamber of Commerce or Better Business Bureau.

Do your own careful "walk around." Are any units for sale? How many, and why? Is the maintenance office on site — or somewhere else?

You, or your lawyer, should then review the condominium declaration and bylaws covering assessments and fees being charged (with special attention to increases), and the insurance or bonding instruments that would protect you in the event of any future financial problems.

Look out for non-specific maintenance "contracts," and avoid voting rules that permit the owner/builder to vote for all non-occupied units, or that give the owner/builder a number of votes for so-called "association assets."

Along with checking records, ask about the rules governing any alterations you might want to make, and about the policies covering your guest privileges, parking, pets, and the use of for-sale signs in the event you decide to move.

If you have any doubts about the upkeep of the property, hire a professional appraiser to inspect it for you.

Meet the People

Condominiums come in all shapes, sizes, and locations —with all kinds of residents and life-styles — and with varying ranges of amenities, from a recreation room with a billiard table to tennis courts and a swimming pool to a recreational universe that includes multiple golf courses. The extras, of course, all carry a price.

Along with making written notes of all the costs, make mental notes of any attempts to high-pressure you into putting yourself under some obligation to buy. Do not sign any papers without reading all the fine print — and don't let anybody shame you into signing up for something you can't afford.

Above all, take time to meet and talk with a cross section of the residents, preferably in a relaxed situation like meal time, to find out what you have in common, and to ask about the people who serve as officers of the condominium association. If possible, meet some of those officers and form your own impressions of how well you would get along with them over time.

Ask Old Friends

Sid Pittman started his adult life by marrying his high school sweetheart, Connie, in Rising Star, Texas. Then he went to Europe, won a Silver Star in one of the most violent actions of World War II, and came back to a career of exploring and drilling for oil in some of the country's most rugged terrain. So it surprised us that the first thing Sid mentioned about his and Connie's new retirement condominium was the 24-hour *security*.

"If you want real carefree living," he wrote recently, "a well-run condominium community like this one is hard to beat. This is great for people who travel a lot and want to be able to come and go without any worries about their home. We're near Granbury, a real picture-book Texas town that reminds us of Rising Star, and we just love the people. If they don't see you for a week or so, someone starts looking for you."

Manufactured Homes

Although the terms seem interchangeable, there is an important technical difference between "mobile" homes and "manufactured" homes. In 1976, Congress passed a law requiring what had been "mobile" homes to meet the U.S. Department of Housing and Urban Development's new "Manufactured Home Construction and Safety Standards" — the "HUD Code" — and to carry a seal certifying code compliance.

The HUD-Code seal, a simple plate like the federal motor vehicle certification plate on the driver's door of your car, means the home is built to federal standards that require more strength, more safety features, and more inspections than are required by many local codes.

Most makers of HUD-Code homes now invite prospective buyers to visit the factories to see for themselves how huge jigs hold the tolerances in structural members to fractions of an inch. Automation, of course, also reduces costs — the makers claim that manufactured housing usually costs about 25 percent less than comparable site-built housing. That's a key reason, they say, why manufactured homes now account for nearly one fourth of U.S. single-family homes.

What About Older Models?

If you look at pre-1976 factory-built homes, pay special attention to the condition of the floors; early-year materials were sometimes vulnerable to moisture. Also, look for telltale stains from leaky roofs, for noticeable "give" and squeaks in wall panels, and for poor-fitting doors and windows. Ideally, talk to a mobile home dealer who specializes in remodeling older homes. For a modest fee, he will make a detailed, professional inspection for you.

As an extra precaution, see if the mobile home you are looking at is listed in the NADA Mobile Home Appraisal Guide, a companion book to the NADA (National Automobile Dealers Association) appraisal book covering used cars.

Above All, Check Location

Whether a factory-built home will hold its value — or gain or lose — will be decided more by its location than its construction. When you buy a factory-built home, you also involve yourself with the park or other community in which the home is located. (In parks, buyers usually order their homes from the various manufacturers through the park owner.)

Most retirees are well aware that the mobile-homers of earlier years were the pioneers of the retirement village concept. According to industry historians Allan D. Wallis, author of *Wheel Estate*, and Peter P. McCormick, it was "Trailer Estates," in Bradenton, Florida, in 1954, that first offered retirees a planned community complete with recreational activities and facilities. Manufactured home communities are now so numerous, and so varied, that choosing the right one for you can be bewildering — unless you follow some basic rules.

Choosing a Park

Before you sign any papers, take time to find out: 1) What can the top local real estate authority — the Board of Realtors — tell you about the history, reputation, and ownership of the park. 2) Are the grounds attractive and well maintained? 3) When you ask the present residents about the park ownership, and about the record of their home owners association, what do they tell you? 4) Do the people you talk with seem to be "your kind of folks" — people who would be congenial neighbors? 5) What kind of utilities, recreational facilities, security features, and other amenities does the park offer, and what is the breakdown of charges? 6) What protection will you have against any unreasonable increase in any of those charges in the future? 7) What are the distances from the park to local restaurants, stores, medical facilities, churches, airports, neighboring cities, and other places of special interest?

Always pick up all the literature a park offers, for comparison with literature from other parks, and to remind you later of some questions you meant to ask — and should.

Never Be Pressured

Moving into a manufactured home community is a giant step. You're not just moving into a new home — you're moving into a new lifestyle. So don't be rushed. If you sign up for any of the "special offers" that could make you feel obligated to sign a contract, will you have enough courage — or just plain gall — to walk away from the obligation? It's your money and you worked hard for it. Remember the dangers of euphoria.

Buy or Rent the Land?

Renting the land means:

- You'll pay only a motor vehicle tax, not property tax.

- On any attachments — patio room, carport, screen porch — you might need to pay an intangible tax.

- If you need financing, you'll pay the regular consumer loan rate.

- The money you would have paid for the land can be invested elsewhere to augment your income.

- If you decide later to move, it might be easier to sell because you would not be selling a lot as well as a home — but this is a point on which many people disagree. And remember that you can't move the home itself without significant expense.

Most states have some regulations covering land-lease communities. Be sure to ask about those regulations before signing any final papers.

Buying the land means: You'll pay property tax, and any financing you need will be at real estate mortgage rates. People who prefer to buy the land, instead of renting, often ask the renters: "Would you build an expensive house on land you did not own?" The question usually generates lively debate.

Final precautions: When purchasing, be sure you understand all details about warranties, terms of sale, delivery time, furnishings to be included in the sale, and any financing involved. Check the "energy package" with special care, because energy packages vary with manufacturers. Above all, make certain the home is properly sited; most long-term mortgages call for "permanent foundations," and as much as 50 percent of all warranty work is directly related to improper setting up and anchoring of the home. Lastly, on delivery day, ask the retailer or contractor who sold you the home to walk through it with you and be a witness to any deficiencies you see.

"Adults Only" Parks

In case you wonder about "Adults Only" signs, here's the background: The Fair Housing Act of 1989 made it illegal to deny housing to families with children, but the law granted an exemption to retiree communities that could meet three major qualifications: 1) At least 80 percent of the homes in the community must have at least one resident over 55. 2) The community must offer significant services and facilities for older people, such as a clubhouse, swimming pool, or classes. 3) The community must have and follow policies that show a clear intent to provide housing for people over 55.

John and Ann McGuire bought a manufactured home in a retirement community after they left Cortland, New York, and they've always been glad they did. "You can get acquainted fast," Ann told us, "if you just get involved in their activities. I volunteered for some assignments and I was soon meeting everybody."

John, a retired marketing professional, agreed the key point was people. "For us, "he said, "this has been a warm, friendly community. When anybody in the place gets sick, the others all come swarming in with food. It would be hard, around here, to feel alone."

9

Adult Congregate Living Facilities

The modern Adult Congregate Living Facility (ACLF) appears under "housing" in this book, instead of under "health," because the ACLF is now the accepted, practical choice of any senior who has (or anticipates having) some health problems, and would like to continue living in homelike surroundings without any sacrifice of independence.

In an earlier age of big families and big houses, a slowing family member was seldom in the way and seldom alone. But now we live in a time when "everybody goes out to work." Inevitably, there came a need for better alternatives to the old familiar (and unfairly stereotyped) nursing home.

Today's assisted living (or "continuous care") facility is typically a cozy, homelike apartment with cheerful freedom and dignified privacy — in an informal social environment of friends and family — and all with a daily wellness check, nutritious meals, and continuing help (if and when needed) with the daily chores of bathing, grooming, walking, and the proper taking of medication.

Flexible Arrangements

Adult Congregate Living Facilities are listed in the Yellow Pages, well known to all local authorities, and closely regulated to ensure high standards of care and value. Today's ACLFs offer a broad choice of accommodations from modest to luxurious, and with a wide range of options in their in-house health care. You can choose a place with six or eight residents, or one with 400 or more, or something in between. You can choose an urban or country locale. You can choose an ACLF with 24-hour supervision by licensed nursing personnel, or one with an adjoining skilled nursing center, or a life-care place. In addition to the assisted living help, some ACLFs offer a wide range of recreational and hobby activities, including indoor aquatic centers and craft rooms.

You also have an extensive choice of payment plans, from monthly rates to yearly lease arrangements to various endowment options. Some also offer rental units. The life-care ACLFs usually offer various refunds in the event you change your mind later about the place and decide to move.

Other Available Options

In surveying today's universe of ACLFs, be sure to consider the many facilities now owned and operated by the various church and fraternal organizations. Also, as part of any thorough review of senior health care options, be sure to update yourself on local day care services offered by your mental health center, and on the growing array of home health care services.

To learn more about ACLFs, ask the Area Aging Agency for a list of local ACLFs and take time to visit the facilities and talk with the people in charge.

Cliff and Donita Paine, in Holland, Michigan, continue to report good health. "But this move," they wrote recently of their move to an ACLF, "was not just for us — it also gives our children a break. The two of us went through a long period of suspense with three of our parents during their declining years, always wondering and worrying about how well they were getting along. It can be traumatic. We don't want to be that kind of burden later to our family."

Living the RV Life

America's newest age of wanderlust living began with a parade of distinguished names. In 1915, President Henry B. Joy of the Packard Motor Car Company asked his craftsmen to build a camping vehicle for him, large enough to provide sleeping and cooking facilities for two people. Henry Ford soon followed suit, along with Thomas Edison. They all liked camping; but not down on the ground.

Four years later, aviator-inventor Glenn Curtiss, who had built the world's first flying boat, brought out his Aerocar, a "motor bungalow" towed by a car. By the mid-twenties, according to industry historians Carlton M. Edwards and Peter P. McCormick, the travel trailer had spawned more than 6,000 "trailer camps" across the United States and the trailer was becoming popular as a seasonal vacation home. By 1940, the over-the-road home reached a fork in its evolution: from that time forward, some would settle on permanent foundations as "mobile homes;" the rest would continue along the open road as "recreational vehicles" or RVs.

Today's RV World

Some 700,000 Americans, according to a study by Dr. Roberta Null of Miami (Ohio) University, are now living the RV life full-time. Ninety percent of those people are over 50, and married, with comfortable incomes. They live in travel trailers (including the long trailer-truck Fifth Wheels), motor homes (including van conversions), campers, and tent trailers — and they live where they please. They have a choice of more than 20,000 commercial campgrounds and RV parks, as well as those on public lands.

The campgrounds and RV resorts have a variety of facilities ranging from wash houses and comfort stations to recreational complexes with swimming pools, tennis courts, and the latest in fitness clubs.

To guide the diverse legions of travelers, the RV industry offers numerous campground directories, magazines and newspapers, and has formed a network of clubs and trade associations.

From their home in Michigan's Irish Hills, near Jackson, retired educators Carlton and Linda Kissner have driven their motor home to all parts of the United States, including Alaska, and have rented RVs in Australia and New Zealand. "We like the freedom of it," they tell us, "but we always advise our friends to rent for a while before they buy. The RV life is not for everybody."

Happily, for those who would like to try before they buy, RV rentals are available throughout the United States.

For more information about the RV life, write to the Recreation Vehicle Industry Association, P.O. Box 2999, Reston, Virginia 22090-0999. Also ask your state tourist bureau about RV facilities, and visit local RV shows and dealerships.

Part III

Making Your Money Last Longer

11

Today Is Day One

Day One of your retirement is an historic starting point, not a finish line, in your financial and other activities. It's a day of getting oriented, a day of becoming fully aware of where you stand.

If you have your net worth statement all prepared and updated, congratulations! If not, don't be dismayed. The Home Economics Office of your County's Cooperative Extension Service can give you a simple form to use, like the one shown on the following page.

Day One of retirement, in a financial sense, can be a bittersweet event. It can come as a blessing, and also as a shock. We are being warned by retirement planners that today's retiree, in an age of upward creep in prices and taxes, will need 60 to 80 percent of his preretirement income just to maintain his general standard of living. Will we be able to make our money last for the rest of our lives?

Many of us, facing the retirement years, are a bit spoiled by the in-house guidance we've had from a professional personnel director and a professional corporate financial officer. Too often, we took their help for granted. Now we have an uneasy feeling of being all-on-our-own.

Sources of Information

Happily, we are surrounded by reliable sources of up-to-date financial information. Here are some examples:

Local banks. Especially if we are in a new area, it's wise to visit at least three banks and compare the completeness of such services as these: savings; checking; safe deposit boxes; trust department services; 24-hour banking; 24-hour account information hotline; investment advice and brokerage service; installment, commercial, and real estate loans; and consolidated monthly statements covering all our transactions. Our personal visits to the banks will help us judge the professionalism of the staffs and their level of interest in meeting our needs. Our bank is not

Net Worth Statement

My Liquid Assets (readily convertible to cash)   Date _____

Cash.. $_____
Bank accounts:
    Checking (a)... $_____
    Savings (a).. $_____
Savings Bonds (d)... $_____
Life Insurance (c)... $_____
Bonds:
    Government (b), Municipal (b)...................... $_____
    Corporate (b)... $_____
Stocks (b), Mutual Funds (b)............................... $_____
Miscellaneous:
    Prepaid taxes... $_____
    Prepaid insurance... $_____
    Other (gold/silver bullion)............................ $_____

My Other Assets

Cash value of company retirement fund........................... $_____
Cash value of private pension plan.................................. $_____
Cash value of profit-sharing plan.................................... $_____
Home (b).. $_____
Other real estate (b).. $_____
Cars (b).. $_____
Personal property (b)... $_____
    silverware, jewelry,... $_____
    furniture, large appliances .... $_____
Other personal property (b)... $_____
    stamp collection, coin collection .... $_____
Investment in antiques, art collection............................ $_____
Debts others owe me.. $_____
Other... $_____

                                      Total Assets $_____

Key: (a) = balance, (b) = market value, (c) = cash surrender value, (d) = current redemption value

Net Worth Statement (Continued)

My Liabilities (debts)

Current debts on:
charge accounts .... $_____
credit cards .... $_____
real estate taxes .... $_____
personal taxes due .... $_____

Installment debts (balance) on:
furniture .... $_____
TV and appliances .... $_____
car .... $_____
other .... $_____

Mortgage debts (home, other real estate)...................... $_____

Miscellaneous loans on:
life insurance policy .... $_____
small business loan .... $_____
other loans .... $_____

Any other outstanding debts .... $_____

Total Liabilities $_____

Net worth equals total assets minus total liabilities

Total Assets $_____
Less Total Liabilities $_____
NET WORTH $_____

Chart courtesy of Florida Cooperative Extension Service

just a nearby, one-stop financial center, it also is a reliable source of re-ferrals to real estate agents, property appraisers, builders, and other people who can be helpful to us.

Social Security and Medicare. Just call 1-800-772-1213 (toll free) for answers to your questions and free booklets on the various services available to you from these federal agencies.

Internal Revenue Service. See page 21 for the toll-free 800 phone numbers of the IRS.

Insurance. Your state insurance department probably offers guid-ance on buying the insurance you need in retirement. Ask your state representative.

U.S. Consumer Information Center offers booklets, free or at mod-est prices, on many subjects of interest to retirees. Send your request for a free catalog to: Consumer Information Center-2A, P.O. Box 100, Pueblo, Colorado 81002.

American Association of Retired Persons (AARP) offers a broad variety of booklets on retiree subjects. See page 22 for information about AARP membership.

Organizing Your Records

Along with starting contacts with your basic sources of continuing in-formation, now is the time to organize your new set of retirement records and store them in safe places.

Legal documents. Birth, marriage, and death certificates; deeds to property; military discharge papers; automobile titles; insurance policies; securities — and all other valuable, hard-to-replace papers — should be kept in a bank safe deposit box.

Financial records. Tax returns for the past six years, product war-ranties — and handy copies of your Power of Attorney and Living Will — should be kept in a metal file drawer in your home.

Entrust your attorney, or a close relative or friend, with your will and codicils, trust papers, copy of Power of Attorney, and final instruc-tions for funeral services. It also is desirable to prepare your own obitu-ary, to be sure all facts are accurate.

In addition to all the above, Day One is the best of times to start tak-ing life one task at a time, one day at a time. Learn to pace yourself like a retiree; you no longer need to be an anxious clock-watcher.

12

Money Management Daily

*T*he basics of successful financial operation at the household level are more easily stated than applied: 1) Never spend more money than you are taking in, and 2) always save some money for a reserve, and for investments.

You recently retired, probably amid a round robin of celebrations, with a whole new kind of first-time freedom and (probably) with a heady feeling of being suddenly rich. That can be a dangerous combination of emotions. In that mood, you are much like the deep-sea diver, long working under pressure, who comes too suddenly to the blue-sky surface. His worry is the bends. Your worry is euphoria.

Starting with Day One, you need to remember that you might be spending nearly half as many years in retirement as you spent on the job — with unpredictable costs ahead and no guarantee of additional wage earning at the old rates.

Needed: New Habits

The good news is that financial security in retirement is mostly a matter of disciplining yourself enough to cultivate some new, thrifty habits and phase out old, wasteful ones. New habits are something you'll need to work at for a while. Give these new habits an honest try and you'll be surprised how soon they become a built-in part of a more secure lifestyle:

Adopt a monthly budget if you don't already have one. The simple form shown on the next page is from the Home Economics Office of our county's Cooperative Extension Service. By the end of three months, you'll know where your carefully-guarded money is going, and you'll see clear indications of where money is being wasted. To make the clues more conspicuous, convert some of the discretionary expenses into percentages from time to time.

In your savings account, try to maintain at least a three month reserve.

Current Income and Expenses

	Month 1	Month 2	Month 3
Income			
Company retirement benefits			
Income from Social Security			
Income from securities			
Income from annuities, rents			
Income from savings			
Other income			
Total Income			
Expenses			
Rent or mortgage			
Utilities			
Installment payments			
Savings			
Insurance			
Transportation			
Food			
Clothing			
Household supplies			
Medical and dental			
Recreation and entertainment			
Miscellaneous			
Total Expenses			
Total Income			
minus Total Expenses			
BALANCE			

Chart courtesy of Florida Cooperative Extension Service

Reevaluate continuing costs, especially credit card purchases and insurance. Interest rates on unpaid credit card balances have run as high as 19.8 percent; keep one major credit card for emergencies, and be sure you're keeping one with the lowest available interest rate.

On insurance, the experts agree that most retirees carry too much; they advise periodic shopping around and comparing policies. In the insurance field, the old conglomeration of hundreds of medigap policies was reduced, in 1992, to a standardized group of ten policies.

Shopping for Savings

Be a comparison shopper. In supermarkets, compare the Per-Oz prices. On general merchandise, compare the prices on major items in two or three discount stores. On prescription drugs, phone three or more pharmacies and find out for yourself how widely the prices can vary — and always ask for generic drugs wherever they are available.

Shop the specials wherever you spend money. Monitor all sales, and the Grand Openings of new stores. Check the Early Bird specials at restaurants. Shop for discounts on movie tickets, transportation, and lodgings. And always remember that coupons are a new form of currency, like cash — one of our friends claims her coupons save her five to ten dollars on every grocery shopping trip. Leading stores often accept the coupons of their competitors; and many churches and charities will appreciate any excess coupons you can give them.

Be a better browser in all the places you visit. Don't always feel obligated to buy something — you now have the luxury of extra time to observe what's new in the world of commerce. Just a little extra browsing can help you stay well informed on an impressive range of practical subjects. You'll be curious enough to notice the bargains in the used appliance and furniture stores, and consignment shops — and you'll discover the new under/wonder world of "Scratch 'n' Dent." (Our newest appliance, with superficial scratches nobody but us would notice, carried a discount of 75 percent.) You also will develop an awareness of what's being offered at the flea markets, garage sales, and yard sales — and will always get there early enough to beat the "regulars," who snap up the special prizes for resale.

Be Energy-Minded

Check the savings you can realize by simply following the tips offered by the U.S. Department of Energy on your insulation, heating and cooling, appliances and lighting. For the newest free booklets, call 1-800-523-2929 (toll free). Also, see if the Home Economics Department of your county's Cooperative Extension Service has any new information about energy use in your own state. All the while, get in the habit of switching off all lights and appliances when you don't really want to push up your light bill.

Switch off faucets as well as switches. Letting hot water run and run is a major waste because water heating represents about 15 percent of all the energy you use in your home. Leaky faucets, over a surprisingly short time, can waste not just hundreds but thousands of gallons of water. Most important of all, in warm climates, find out how much outdoor water you're using. One sunbelt city found that 50 percent of all its water was going into lawn sprinkling — and that 50 percent of that lawn water was being wasted by mid-day use under a hot sun. Environmental authorities have been warning us that water is on its way to becoming as expensive as electricity and that more of us should start xeriscaping our yards. We should listen.

Combine car trips. Keep an errand list on hand and try to cover two or more every time you take the car out. Also, learn to drive more slowly: the average car uses about 15 percent less fuel at 55 mph than at 65 mph. Best of all, try to do more of your nearby shopping by bicycle or tricycle — or even by foot, with a cart. Remember when people did things like that every day?

Reuse and recycle. It's a national program that begins with conscientious people like us. Try always to use paper towels more than once; share magazines with your neighbors; donate used items to people in need. Recycle newspapers, aluminum beverage cans, all glass containers, and plastic bottles.

Time your phone calls. Telephones, for retirees, can be lifelines — essential connections with family, friends, and daily needs. But the talk is not always cheap. When Fred and Elke Forbes of Wilmington, Delaware, began their retirement with a second-for-each marriage, their family expanded instantly to two daughters and five sons in seven different locations, including one in Europe. Elke, the ultimate in loving mothers, kept in close touch with them all. By phone.

One of the subsequent phone bills had her almost in tears. "This," she complained to us (over the phone), "is unbelievable — it's in the *hundreds!* I don't know what I can do about this, but I'll have to do *something*."

Elke did. The next phone call brought happy news: "I've found an easy way to keep my long distance calls under control. Fred found it at our electronics store. It's called a 'countdown timer.' You set a time limit for your call, and the countdown timer begins beeping when your time is up. They say it's also good for cooking, and for timing medication. You might like one for yourselves."

13

Money Management Yearly

*H*ere, on the facing page, you have a simplified, at-a-glance view of the vast and complex universe of investments, with the lowest risks at the bottom and the highest risks at the top.

Our advisers in retirement areas have told us that retirees tend to consolidate their holdings in the bottom two portions of the pyramid, with monthly income as a primary concern. Many investors then move upward in the pyramid, in order to keep pace with inflation, and begin to buy mutual funds, which offer diversification with a variety of orientations, such as stocks, bonds, and money-market funds.

To whom should a retiree turn for wise advice on investing, with all its inherent and constantly-changing risks?

Get Professional Advice

When we once asked our friend Jim Calby for some investment guidance, he quickly declined, politely but firmly. Jim had been a top corporate financial officer in Dayton, Ohio. "Look," he said, "I wouldn't dare give you any advice because I don't know your individual situation. You need a professional planner, somebody who is totally independent, with nothing to sell. Tell him everything about your finances and your goals. Pay him a fee. Keep away from the rainbow salesmen."

The much-publicized John Templeton, often quoted in *The Wall Street Journal* and sometimes called "the greatest of all stock pickers," once said the basics of investing are diversification, flexibility, and patience. He described his own formula as "Be frugal, start slowly, build carefully, and use common sense."

Our own confidential adviser, who holds an M.B.A. degree and has an impressive background in the financial field, is an old and trusted friend as well as a professional financial planner, and he knows every detail of our financial history.

The Investment Risk Pyramid

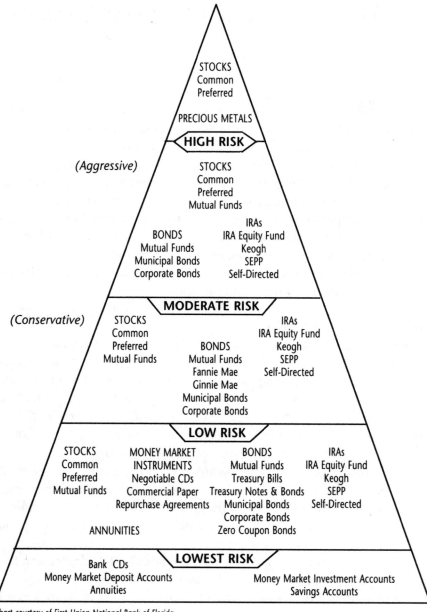

(Aggressive)

(Conservative)

STOCKS
Common
Preferred

PRECIOUS METALS

HIGH RISK

STOCKS
Common
Preferred
Mutual Funds

BONDS
Mutual Funds
Municipal Bonds
Corporate Bonds

IRAs
IRA Equity Fund
Keogh
SEPP
Self-Directed

MODERATE RISK

STOCKS
Common
Preferred
Mutual Funds

BONDS
Mutual Funds
Fannie Mae
Ginnie Mae
Municipal Bonds
Corporate Bonds

IRAs
IRA Equity Fund
Keogh
SEPP
Self-Directed

LOW RISK

STOCKS
Common
Preferred
Mutual Funds

**MONEY MARKET
INSTRUMENTS**
Negotiable CDs
Commercial Paper
Repurchase Agreements

BONDS
Mutual Funds
Treasury Bills
Treasury Notes & Bonds
Municipal Bonds
Corporate Bonds
Zero Coupon Bonds

IRAs
IRA Equity Fund
Keogh
SEPP
Self-Directed

ANNUITIES

LOWEST RISK

Bank CDs
Money Market Deposit Accounts
Annuities

Money Market Investment Accounts
Savings Accounts

Chart courtesy of First Union National Bank of Florida

He echoed our question, "To what extent do retirees need professional financial planning help?" His response: "There's no single, simple answer to that.

"Many retirees," he continued, "just have a couple of burning questions they should take to the accountant who prepares their taxes. If they want a comprehensive plan, of course, I advise them to talk to a (CFP) — a Certified Financial Planner. The CFP may offer one-time suggestions for a flat fee, or may offer to help with the implementation of a comprehensive program for a management fee, based on a percentage of the assets involved. Once that plan has been put in place, there should be little need for a broker to turn assets frequently.

"In any event," he concluded, "retirees should remember that many brokers who represent themselves as 'financial planners' are really financial product salesmen who are being paid to generate *transactions*."

Choosing a Financial Planner

As part of its Consumer Information Series, the Council of Better Business Bureaus, Inc., offers a highly informative publication, *Tips on Financial Planners*. To receive a free copy, send your request, and $1.00 for postage and handling, payable to the Council of Better Business Bureaus, Department 023, Washington, DC 20042-0023. Enclose a self-addressed, business-size envelope.

The BBB guide explains the qualifications needed for all these titles used by financial planners:

- CFP - Certified Financial Planner.
- CHFC - Chartered Financial Consultant.
- MSFS - Master of Science in Financial Services.
- MBA - Masters Degree in Business Administration.
- Registry of Financial Planning Practitioners.

The Council of Better Business Bureaus, and Better Business Bureaus throughout the country, do not endorse or recommend any product, service, or company, including financial products and institutions. With that guarantee of neutrality, the BBB takes you through the preliminary steps in choosing the finalists for your financial planning assignment, and then suggests that you ask each candidate these questions:

What is your professional background? Look for a strong track record of education and job experience covering a broad spectrum of financial planning needs.

How long have you been a financial planner? Look for three or more years of experience as a financial planner, and several more years of prior experience as a broker, insurance agent, accountant, or lawyer.

Will you provide references? Get the names of three or more clients whom the planner has counseled for at least two years. Ask them about their level of satisfaction, their investment returns, and their intentions of staying with the financial planner.

May I see examples of plans and monitoring reports you have drawn up for other investors? Pay particular attention to the frequency and quality of the monitoring reports, since these updates will be vital to reviewing and recharting your financial objectives.

Will I be dealing with you or with an associate? If your planner will be turning over much of the work on your financial plan to an associate, take the time to check out that individual.

What specific experience do you have in the areas that concern me? Some planners specialize in one or more areas of financial planning, or in a certain type of client. In such a case, determine whether an area of specialty matches your goals.

After you have selected a financial planner, our friends among the experts advise you to keep yourself informed on the fast-changing financial world by reading such periodicals as *The Wall Street Journal, Barron's, Kiplinger's Personal Finance Magazine*, and *Money Magazine*.

Estate Planning

Back in Chapter 11, we mentioned your will as one of the important documents you should store with care. Now we should point out that your will is the very first document needed in any estate-planning program. If you do not leave a will, your state will appoint an administrator (who will be paid from your estate) to distribute your estate in accordance with state inheritance laws.

Most retirees made their wills long ago; but not all of those wills are up to date and valid.

A will, the experts tell us, should be reviewed at least once a year to be sure it has kept up with changes in your resources, your choice of beneficiaries, and your place of residence. If you moved to another state after retiring, you probably need to update your will.

Along with a valid will, you are advised to have three additional documents:

- Living Trust

- Living Will

- Durable Power of Attorney

A living trust (like various other trust plans) gives you better control over the distribution of your estate in many ways, but its principal advantage is this: it lets you avoid probate. The probate process is costly and time-consuming, and it applies in each and every state in which you own property.

A living will is a medical consideration: it instructs doctors to relieve pain but not to prolong life with any artificial methods when death is imminent.

A durable power of attorney is more specific than a general power of attorney: its purpose is to make sure your wishes are carried out in the event you are incapacitated, and it must carry a statement to that effect.

Getting the Right Guidance

Depending on the size and complexity of your estate, you may or may not need the professional services of a lawyer and a financial planner. In many cases, a current do-it-yourself legal guidebook will answer most of your questions. Two such guidebooks are *Legal-Wise: Self-Help Legal Forms for Everyone* and *Senior Counsel: Legal and Financial Advice for Age 50 and Beyond,* both published by Allworth Press, New York.

In the event you decide you need professional legal services, good guidance in choosing a lawyer is available from the referral service of your local or state bar association.

14

Do You Want a Job?

"**N**o retirement program is complete," the professional planner told us, "unless it includes a *salable skill*. There's no telling when you might want, or need, some sort of job.

"You start," he said, "by making a list, on a sheet of paper, of all your experience, skills, and aptitudes — and then asking your family and friends to suggest additions and changes, including some possible cuts. Next, take a good look at the local job market and see how well you can match up your list of qualifications against what's available out there."

The Job Universe

Today's working world is a massive collection of more than 250 active occupations, with some 35,000 job titles, and most of them are always undergoing some evolutionary change — but don't be intimidated by all those numbers. Happily for the retiree, both male and female, the principal categories boil down to only a dozen clusters, and then down again to these half-dozen fields of special interest to retirees:

Administrative support. This is the largest occupational group, encompassing office workers of all kinds.

Marketing and sales. This field, which includes retail stores, is characterized by high turnover and a high percentage of part-time jobs.

Mechanics, installers, repairers. These skills are needed to maintain all the mechanical and electronic equipment.

Services. Food and beverage service, security guards, cleaning, lawn care, and personal services — they're all here, all supported by the age of increasing leisure time.

Professional specialties. Computer specialists, health care givers, and teachers are in this category.

Construction trades. The nation needs help building new structures and rehabilitating old ones. Some of the work may be too rugged for retirees; but power tools can ease the strain.

Use Your Resources

To guide you in matching your qualifications to the jobs out there, turn to the resources that are waiting to help:

- State Job Service. Your state office is linked with the U.S. Department of Labor's Employment Service, with some 2,000 local employment centers, whose purpose is to match up applicants with employers. Your job service office will show you how to prepare a resume and conduct a job interview, at no charge to you.

- Senior Center. Local senior centers often offer job leads and sponsor senior job fairs.

- Classified ads. Read them all; but be wary of "blind" ads with little or no sponsor identification, and "no experience needed" ads — they often mean low wages, poor working conditions, or straight commission work.

- Employment agencies. In dealing with any private, commercial job service, be sure you are fully aware of all fees and other charges. Be suspicious of any firm that wants cash for job leads, which are sometimes disguised as "value-added data."

- Labor unions and professional associations are good sources of job leads.

- Your vo-tech center and community college are important contacts in any thorough job search. They keep in close touch with local employer needs and gear many courses to those needs. So, if you lack a salable skill, it's probably within your reach at vo-tech or the college.

Age Is Not a Problem

Anybody who looks for a job must be prepared for many rejections. After all, he or she is trying to sell a person, and a person is a highly specialized product for which there is seldom a universal demand. But at least the climate for job-hunting retirees is improving. Population trends (fewer children and longer-living adults) and the federal Age Discrimination in Employment Act (which protects workers of 40 to 70) have improved the public attitude toward older workers. So age is not the problem it once was.

Neither is gender. World War II brought an army of women into the workplace, and they are thriving there. By the year 2000, women are expected to account for about half of all the jobs.

Major employers, here and there, have been accelerating the improvement of the image of older workers. A significant example of that
is the experience, in Florida, of the Publix Supermarket chain. Florida
has a higher percentage of retirees than any other state, and Publix, for
many years, has been hiring so many retirees that many have now passed
the 80 mark and are still going strong.

The Publix "Prime Timers"

In the beginning, the Publix interest in retirees was simply a business-
like response to two demographic facts: 1) The declining birth rate of
more than 20 years had created a critical shortage of the teens who once
filled traditional after-school and weekend jobs. 2) The national shift
from goods-producing to service-producing industries was creating a
whole new generation of part-time jobs that needed to be filled.

Retirees were a natural, obvious answer to both problems. Publix
began hiring and training seniors the same as everybody else and everything moved along smoothly.

But then the Publix Human Resources Department began to notice a
surprising change in the spirit of their large and diverse family of "associates." They launched a special study and soon proved to themselves that
"young people who work alongside older people perform better than those
who don't." The older people — now nicknamed the "prime timers" — were
providing a sense of stability and dedication to getting the job done, while
the younger people were providing an abundance of energy and enthusiasm.

Publix management now refers to the new mix as "a wonderful chem-
istry" they would hate to be without.

The Publix prime timers are a diverse group: a retired accountant
who always wanted more chances to "meet the public"... a police chief
who was "bored stiff" in retirement ... a retired receptionist, now a dem-
onstrator, who likes to help people plan their meals ... the retired owner
of a manufacturing company who likes to see happy children around a
store. No two are alike. So what was the *salable skill* they offered Publix?

"In retailing," says Publix, "our most important job is being a cheerful
servant to our customers. Our people learn to regard themselves as professionals in customer relations."

But why did these retirees apply for jobs in the first place—Did they
just want something to do, or did they *need* the jobs for financial
or other reasons?

Was It "Want" or "Need"?

To those who like to understand the workings of the retiree mind, here are some timely thoughts from a letter one retiree wrote to Publix management. The letter writer had operated a successful business of his own for 30 years.

"This job creates in me a sense of belonging to a team," he wrote. "I benefit from the dignity and consideration that exists between the management and the associates.

"Most importantly," he continued, "it keeps alive within me a value of self-worth, of being needed, of a job being well done. I believe one of the most devastating feelings one finds in retirement is that of not being needed. Working part-time has kept alive the feeling of being needed — and the satisfaction of knowing I can still get the job done the way an important company would like the job to be done."

15

Starting Your Own Business

Dream about it as much as you like — but before you put any of your hard-earned **CASH** into that new business venture, ask yourself these questions about it:

1. Will your product or service meet a presently-unserved need in your area?
2. Will you be serving an existing market in which demand exceeds supply?
3. Will you be able to compete successfully with existing businesses serving the same market niche?
4. Have you estimated, in detail, what your operating costs will be for your first two years?
5. Have you had personal, hands-on experience in all the basic operations of the business you're thinking of entering?

These questions come from the specialists of the U.S. Small Business Administration (SBA) and the Service Corps of Retired Executives (SCORE).

"More than seventy percent of all new business start-ups will fail within the first year," says one SCORE volunteer, "and the two main reasons will be that they don't know the business and they don't have enough capital."

Start Slow...But Sure
Along with the questions about the business, ask yourself some objective questions about your own motivations. You are now a retiree, and retirees tend to want one more turn at bat, one last hurrah, one final chance to grab the brass ring. Be bluntly honest with yourself: could your idea for a new business of your own be called an "ego trip"? A desperate "get rich-quick" idea? A case of "being played for a sucker by a slick promoter"? If you have to say yes to any of those questions, better think some more before you leap.

But if your venture relates to a field in which you have served an apprenticeship and really know your way around—and if you have a *well-thought-out way of doing something better in that field* — then *go for it!*

Obviously, you should think first of just continuing the kind of work you've always done, but now as a supporting arm —a subcontractor to a going business. You can easily set yourself up as a proprietorship with your own occupational license. Whatever move you decide to make, move one slow, sure step at a time. Here are some of the steps you should take:

Marketing Research

Research is just a matter of finding answers to questions. Some of the answers you need are already waiting for you, in print. Other answers are waiting for you in the heads of other people. The local Yellow Pages offer you a quick overview of your area's commercial universe. Then ask, at your library, to see a copy of the *U.S. Industrial Outlook* (published by the U.S. Department of Commerce), which will tell you what's happening all over America in some 250 industries. Also, at your library, ask for a directory of trade journals, which cover more than 150 different business fields in a continuing, in-depth way. Take down some names and addresses and plan to write to certain publishers for their comments about the latest developments in their fields. (Trade journals can be gold mines of up-to-date information.)

Along with your letters to trade journals, write for a free catalog from the U.S. Consumer Information Center (P.O. Box 100, Pueblo, CO 81002). The Center offers a choice of booklets on starting and managing a business; the booklets are free, or modestly priced.

After briefing yourself with your basic reading, talk with some people who have a face-to-face, working knowledge of local business: the advertising managers of your local newspaper and the broadcast stations. Also invite comments at the Chamber of Commerce. You don't need to reveal your plans — just introduce yourself as a person who is thinking of investing in a new business. The people you talk to will usually feel complimented to be asked for their opinions.

Expert Counseling

Now you're ready to talk specifics — openly, but on a confidential basis — with counselors from the Small Business Administration and its SCORE volunteers, and from your local community college and vocational-technical center. Take advantage of personal interviews, seminars, and training courses—all modestly priced, with even some free help.

Ask the experts for their advice on such considerations as your place of business, the ways of promoting your business, and whether you should become a proprietorship or a corporation or some other kind of business entity.

New businesses usually sprout best in modest, humble places—not in palatial offices but in kitchens and garages and even mini-warehouse units with pull-cord lights; not in showplace malls but in small, strip shopping centers. And they usually grow best when they promote themselves selectively — not with mass media but with simple signs, flyers, and ads in the local neighborhood shopper papers.

Ask Other Retirees

Every retiree community has a "brain trust" available to you for the asking. A good way to find those wise ones is simply to "ask around" at the Senior Center. Meanwhile, here are some observations from a few trusted retiree friends of ours:

Aldis Butler of San Francisco ranks as one of America's top advertising executives, with special expertise in franchise operations. "The word franchise," he always points out, "is an old one, and it simply means a special right or privilege. The most familiar franchise-holders are automobile dealers. They have the exclusive right to sell certain cars in certain territories, and it takes a lot of know-how and hard work for a car dealer to be successful. It's a shame that so many people now think a franchise is a quick ticket to easy riches.

"Too many franchise applicants fail to ask the most basic questions: How stable and profitable is the *market*? How experienced and honorable are the promoters? What percentage of my profit will they be collecting? What will they be doing for me that I couldn't do as well — and cheaper — for myself? Too many people rush into places where they've never served an apprenticeship and don't really know their way around. So they often get burned."

Along with his cautions about franchise operations, Aldis offers some comments about ads for opportunities in multilevel or network marketing organizations. He notes that *network marketing* can often be suspiciously close to *pyramid schemes,* which are illegal in many states. In both types of marketing, an individual can buy a kit of products to sell door-to-door. He thus becomes a *distributor* who can buy at wholesale and sell at retail. He also can make extra commissions by recruiting other distributors. To anyone seeking a business of his own, it's an attractive way to be in business without paying somebody a big franchise fee.

So what's the basic difference between a legitimate multilevel/network marketing operation and a questionable pyramid scheme? "The difference," Aldis explains, "is a subtle one: In legitimate multilevel marketing, the participants have some incentive to recruit new members, but the main emphasis is on selling products. In a pyramid scheme, it's the other way around: there is little or no emphasis on selling products and heavy emphasis on recruiting new members. In some past pyramid schemes, a few promoters at the top made fortunes while many so-called distributors at the bottom wound up with an expensive inventory of products nobody wanted."

Author's note: Anyone who is confused about multilevel/network ads is advised to contact the nearest Better Business Bureau. As an additional precaution, contact the Direct Selling Association, 1776 K Street, N.W., Washington, DC 20006-2387.

Roger Manning of Chicago headed a national media-buying organization. "Anybody who wants to promote a new business," he says, "should be aware that the first rule about buying advertising time and space is: *be important where you are.* The average franchise-holder, or participant in a multilevel marketing operation, is often overly impressed by a promise of heavy advertising support in television and newspapers. He should update himself on two significant media facts:

"First, television is no longer dominated by a few networks; it has been splintered by dozens of cable channels. Second, newspaper carriers no longer just deliver the newspaper — they have become *carrier systems* for delivering many other promotional materials that used to go by mail. The result of those developments is that the visibility of commercials and ads can be reduced. Before anyone invests money in advertising, he should find out which medium reaches the highest concentration of his prospects at the lowest cost per thousand prospects. Always remember: the name of the game is to reach *prospects,* not just everybody."

Ed Hadley went from Cincinnati to the Air Force, then into piloting for a major airline. When a failed eye test ended his flying, he ran his own successful transmission shop. When he married Lori, who was fashion-wise and liked selling, they opened a women's fashion store in a smart resort area. Now he advises other would-be merchants: "Know your product, know your competition, be sure you have a good profit margin — and have at least three years' operating capital.

"And if it's a retail store, your choice of location will either make you or break you. This is hard work for both of us—buying the right goods at the right prices, planning displays and sales, being on the alert for shoplifters, getting and holding reliable help, and keeping the books. But this is our own business. We started it, we know how to run it, and we don't have to share our profits with anyone else."

John McAlpine of Detroit had budgeting as one of his career responsibilities in giant corporations and small start-ups. Now he tells us: "Opening a new business is quite easy — but *keeping* it open is something else. The first thoughts of anybody who wants to start a new business should be about capital. Start-up costs and cash flow. Capital is the element that causes more stress, more arguments, more sleepless nights, and more of everything unpleasant. Retirees, in my experience, can become more stressed and agitated about finances than younger people, and this often leads to panic, or near-panic, and to some faulty and even disastrous decisions."

Our wise, experienced friends tend to agree: "Instead of becoming the owner and chief executive, with all its responsibilities and extra work, you might be glad later that you settled for a spot as a senior partner, investor, or just advisor."

16

Cons, Scams, and Swindles

*I*n an age when we think we know a lot about crime in all its forms, some of the most persistent and insidious offenses are seldom reported. Confidence games — also known as cons, scams, swindles, and rip-offs — are being played over our telephones, through our mail, and at our doors. The cheating has now reached these proportions:

- Telemarketing fraud alone has touched more than 90 percent of all Americans, has victimized more than one in four of them, and retirees are among the most vulnerable.

- One key reason why the threat is growing is that only one victim in 10,000 reports the crime. The others are too ashamed to admit they acted so foolishly — so they remain silent and just let the crooks go on to prey on someone else.

Here are some typical examples of what we should be watching out for:

- A postcard arrives in our mail with the good news that we have won a fabulous prize. All we need to do to claim it is call a 900 number. We do. We talk to an operator who asks for a lot of information, including a credit card number, to "verify" our eligibility. To remain "eligible," we may also be required to buy certain products. The prize never arrives, but we get a bill for the 900 call and the crooks have our credit card number.

- We receive a phone call from a nice man we met recently in one of our civic gatherings. He is calling for a charitable organization, asking for a donation for a local hardship case we hadn't heard about but probably should have. The story is so tragic it almost has us in tears, and the need is so urgent there is no time to spare. The nice man says he will send his wife around to pick up our check.

- The man on the phone says he is a bank examiner. In strict confidence, he tells us he needs our help to catch a crooked employee in our bank who has been stealing from customer accounts and may soon be stealing from ours. He seems to know a lot about our bank; he even mentions our account number. He needs a certain sum of cash from our account so that the bills can be marked in a special FBI way. We are to meet him, and a plainclothes detective who will be with him, and he will give us an official receipt for the money.

- The man at our door offers to resurface our broken driveway for a fraction of what it normally would cost because he has a large quantity of asphalt left over from another job. He will do the job tomorrow, but he needs the money in advance for some repairs to his truck. He looks like a hard worker.

We can't believe we fell for something like that — but we did. And we're far from being alone. Confidence games run through investment offers, land bargains, service contracts, left-over merchandise we can have if we act fast — the list covers everything in the world of bargains.

How to Protect Yourself

Always say no and hang up on suspicious calls.

- Always ask questions about any proposition that might be honest but is being offered by strangers.

- Never give out information over the phone about any confidential number: Social Security, credit card, bank accounts. (And never mention any such numbers in a public place — like an open phone booth — where you can be overheard by strangers.)

- Never respond to any "free" offer that requires you to buy something or to call a 900 number.

- Never invest in anything without seeing references and a prospectus.

- Never donate to any charity you are not familiar with.

- Never order repairs from a stranger whose identity is unknown to you, and never pay for work until it is completed to your satisfaction. Under law, contractors are required to give you written cost estimates for all work — and you have three business days during which you can invoke your Right of Recision, and cancel everything.

Further Action to Take

After hanging up on suspicious calls, please report them to the nearest Better Business Bureau, or to the Consumer Protection Agency of your city or county, or to the state attorney general's office. Do this not only for your own future protection, but to help protect others. These organizations are compiling evidence about cons, scams, and swindles, and they are succeeding in bringing the crooks to justice — often in ways you never hear about.

If somebody has taken any of your money through a deceptive practice, report it immediately to the police.

If the police say it's doubtful you could get your money back (perhaps because your gullibility permitted the crime to happen), ask for help from a television station that has a reporter assigned to cover cases of fraud.

If a fraudulent item was charged to your credit card, report it immediately to your credit card issuer. They may forgive the charge.

If a 900 number was involved, report it to your long-distance phone company. They may cancel the charge.

Remember Two Rules

For years, the Better Business Bureaus have been advising consumers: "Before you invest, investigate," and "If it seems too good to be true, it probably is." Following those two rules is your simplest defense against the cons, scams, and swindles.

The Better Business Bureaus are supported by reputable businesses that have made a commitment to uphold ethical business practices. Better Business Bureaus do not recommend or endorse any company, product, or service, but will give you a reliability report on any company you inquire about.

Part IV

Helping Yourself to Health

Welcome to the
Age of Living Longer

*F*or more than 80 percent of the American population, according to our National Institutes of Health, today's life expectancy is beyond the age of 70.

This is the age of preventive medicine — an age of screening programs and wellness programs and self-help programs. No longer can we afford, as a nation, to let small, neglected health problems grow into catastrophic crises.

After an early-warning screening, and the conditioning of wellness programs, continued health maintenance will rely on a triangular defense system of personal hygiene, regular exercise, and new-age nutrition.

Hygiene Made Early History
Personal hygiene made some of the first major contributions to longevity. Improvements in personal hygiene — with big assists from vaccinations and antibiotics — are given most of the credit for the extending of life expectancy from around 50 years, in 1900, to about 75 years by the 1980s. Surprisingly, one of the most significant advances in hygiene came with the discovery that more germs are transmitted by unclean hands than in any other way.

Hygienists found that, on a square-inch basis, there are more germs under and around fingernails than anywhere else on the body. Thus, when we catch colds, we probably get them from someone who has the virus on his hands, or from touching something that person has touched within the last day or two. It may sound ridiculously simple, but one of the most important rules of good health is: *wash your hands!*

Exercise — Two Ways
Regular exercise, for retirees, divides into two programs: 1) Brisk, aerobic exercise that improves heart and lung action (examples: jogging,

rapid walking, bicycling, swimming). 2) Moderate exercise that strengthens muscles and improves flexibility (examples: calisthenics, yard work, lifting light weights).

Aerobic (connoting oxygen) exercise, which speeds up our heart rate and deepens our breathing, should be performed for about 20 minutes at a time, three times a week. Moderate exercise should be performed for about one hour every day.

The best way to start any exercise program, the experts agree, is with a daily round of walking.

Exercise will be covered in more detail in later chapters.

Nutrition for Seniors

The U.S. Department of Agriculture revolutionized our eating habits in 1992 with the introduction of its Food Guide Pyramid and Dietary Guidelines, designed to shift us to low-fat, low-calorie, high-fiber foods, with five daily servings of fruits and vegetables, and only two 3-ounce portions of meat per day. Please refer to a later chapter, "Eating Right," for the complete story on the new dietary guidelines.

The "Eating Right" chapter covers the seven dietary guidelines, offers recommendations on health-oriented cookbooks, and includes tips on healthier ways of eating out. It also deals with a number of special nutrition problems among retirees and presents solutions to those problems.

Risk Factors

Refer now to Dr. Louis J. Radnothy's simple chart summarizing the risk factors we all face. Note how many of the risk factors are alterable — factors we can control, and change for the better, if we just make up our minds to do so.

Your own physician is a good person to turn to for explanations of any points you do not understand.

Risk Factors

Non-Alterable

Age
Heredity
Gender (women live longer)

Alterable

Dietary
  High Cholesterol (above 200)
  Low HDL Cholesterol (below 35)
  High Blood Sugar
  High Triglycerides
  High Uric Acids
  High Calories (obesity 20% or more over Ideal Body Weight)
  Alcohol Consumption (more than 2 oz. per day)

Habits
  Cigarette Smoking
  Caffeine Abuse
  Sedentary Lifestyle
  Type A Personality Stress

Other
  Lack of Estrogen (women)
  High Blood Pressure (over 150/90)
  Left Ventricular Hypertrophy

Chart courtesy of Louis J. Radnothy, D.O., F.A.C.G.P,

Screening Programs

By definition, Preventive Medicine begins with *Primary* Preventive activities, notably health education, begun by parents with infants and continued through kindergarten and all the higher grades — and then through lifelong learning. Primary preventive activities all take place prior to the onset of illness or injury.

Then come *Secondary* Preventive activities that screen for illness or injury in early stages. Screenings are followed, in turn, by *Tertiary* Preventive activities — such as physical therapy for arthritic patients — which try to limit the disability of existing illness or injury.

All leading hospitals — even in small towns — now offer an increasingly wide choice of screening programs and wellness (tertiary) programs, and educational lectures, to cover the full range of preventive medicine. Here is a sampling of the screening programs available to us — free or modestly priced — at hospitals within a 30-minute drive of our small-town home.

- Blood pressure

- Blood sugar test for diabetes

- Cancer — screening for breast, colorectal, prostate, and skin cancer

- Cholesterol

- Glaucoma

- Grip strength and flexibility

- Hearing

- Nutritional information

- Peripheral vascular disease

- Pulmonary function

- Sleep disorders

- Vision

Wellness Programs

As practiced by leading hospitals, today's wellness programs include the primary prevention of education, the secondary prevention of screenings, and the tertiary prevention that tries to limit the disabling effects of an existing health problem.

Then the wellness programs go a step further. They strive to put people into the best possible physical condition, because people in top condition will bounce back faster from later health threats than will people whose fitness has been neglected.

Here are some examples of wellness programs — all modestly priced — at hospitals within a 30-minute drive from our home.

Basic Wellness Program — provides these services:

- Lifestyle/risk factor analysis
- Blood cardiac risk profile
- Fitness evaluation (including pulmonary function test)
- Nutritional analysis
- Personal interview with Registered Dietitian
- Individualized nutritional and exercise guidelines
- Four-month supervised fitness program
- Two-month re-evaluation
- Continuing health promotion seminars
- Access to scheduled aquacize and aerobic classes

Aquacize Program — follows the guidelines of the Arthritis Foundation. Aquatic exercises promote increased flexibility and muscular strength without putting undue stress on the joints. In addition, the aquacize program offers an enjoyable way to strengthen the cardiovascular system by providing exercise to music.

Aerobics Program — offers low-impact, step-bench, body shaping, and exercise combination classes. The classes are taught by certified aerobics instructors who conduct the exercises to music.

Swim Only Program — offers use of the heated swimming pool, whirl-pool, and sauna six days a week. The swimming pool may be used for water walking, lap swimming, or personal exercises.

Continence Program — evaluates bladder control problems and gives people individual treatment plans for biofeedback, electrical muscle stimulation, and continuing exercise.

Weight Loss Program — closely supervised fitness activity combining nutritional and exercise guidelines and the use of such apparatus as a rowing machine, bicycle, and stairclimber. One woman lost 30 pounds in the first month, and a total of 75 pounds in one year, and has learned how to keep her weight down. She has gone from a size 20 to a size 4, and her percentage of body fat has gone from 35 percent to 21 percent.

20

Same-Day Surgery

You come in for a preoperative visit, arranged by your physician, and complete any tests and x-rays that may have been ordered. You also complete some medical history forms and receive a briefing on what to anticipate during your same-day surgery.

On surgery day, you'll come in at least one hour in advance. A visitor may stay with you before and after surgery. In about one to three hours after surgery, you should be ready to go home. If you have received anesthesia, you will want a responsible adult to drive you.

Here are some examples of the same-day surgical procedures and specialties available to us within a 30-minute drive from our home. They all help bring down the costs of health care.

General Surgery and Endoscopies

- Breast biopsy, with or without lumpectomy and axillary node dissection, or implantation of radiation carrier for loading at a later time.

- Hernia operations: inguinal, umbilical, and others.

- Skin lesions.

- Lymph node biopsies.

- Laparoscopic cholecystectomies.

- Endoscopic procedures: bronchoscopy, colonoscopy, gastroscopy, and others.

- Insertion of indwelling catheters and infusion ports for long-term medication therapy.

- Hemorrhoidectomy and other rectal procedures.

Ear-Nose-Throat Surgery

- Tonsils, adenoids.
- Myringotomies.
- Esophagoscopy.
- Bronchoscopy.
- Skin lesions, with or without reconstruction.
- Lymph node disection.
- Biopsies and excisions.
- Septoplasty/rhinoplasty.
- Otoplasties.
- Tympanoplasty.
- Stapedectomy.
- Sinus surgery.

Plastic/Reconstruction Surgery

- Facelifts, browlifts, blepharoplasty.
- Otoplasties.
- Rhino/septoplasty.
- Breast augmentation, mastopexy, breast reduction (selected cases).
- Skin lesions, with or without reconstruction.
- Skin grafts.
- Hand surgery (selected cases).
- Vein stripping.
- Suction lipectomy.

Orthopedic Surgery

- Carpal tunnels and other minor hand surgery.
- Selective fracture reductions, including pins and plaster.
- Corrective surgery for such problems as bunions and hammertoes.
- Bone biopsies.
- Arthroscopy for temporomandibular joint syndrome (TMJ).
- Arthroscopy for knee and shoulder.
- Superficial soft tissue lesions.
- Y&D infections.
- Reduction of dislocations.

Ophthalmology

- Cataract surgery.
- Eyelid surgery.
- Tear duct surgery.
- Eye muscle surgery.
- Glaucoma surgery.
- Penetrating deratoplasty and other corneal procedures.

Urology

- Kidney stone blasting.
- Cystoscopies, with or without biopsies, stents, laser cautery.
- Hydrocelectomy.
- Orchiectomy.
- Circumcision.
- Lithotripsy.
- UR-BT (intermediate).
- Laser bladder neck contractures.
- Penile condylomata.
- TUR VNC.
- Ureteroscopy, with or without stone basketing.
- Balloon dilatation of prostate.

Obstetrics/Gynecology

- D&C, D&E.
- Tubal ligation.
- Diagnostic laparoscopy.
- Hysteroscopy.
- Surgical laparoscopy.
- Minor vulvar and vaginal procedure.

Dentistry

- Dental restoration.
- Dental extraction.
- Dental surgery.

21

Keeping Up with Medicare

*M*edicare is a federal health insurance plan for people who are 65 and older, and for certain disabled people. It has two parts:

Hospital insurance — Part A. This pays for part of your in patient hospital care and certain follow-up services. You are not charged a premium for Part A, but you are expected to pay for various services it does not cover.

Medical insurance — Part B. This coverage is optional and you will be charged a monthly premium for it. You also must pay an annual deductible, and 20 percent of the amount Medicare approves for each of your medical bills. If you have supplementary ("medigap") health insurance, it will usually cover this 20 percent difference. Note: not all physicians will accept Medicare assignments and abide by Medicare rates; so be sure your physician will accept a Medicare assignment before you incur any charges.

Working together, Parts A and B of Medicare insurance have been a solid help to seniors — but not a big enough help. Together, Parts A and B paid for less than half of the seniors' total health care bill. There was a critical need, early on, for insurance coverage to supplement Medicare coverage and fill what came to be known as the "medigap."

Medigap Insurance

Private insurance companies rushed in to fill the "medigap," and ultimately their array of policies ran into the hundreds. Confusion, for the insurance buyer, was formidable. Happily, the problem demanded and brought reform: Medicare supplement policies were in time limited to 10 standard benefit packages.

Another major reform appeared in 1992, when a new kind of Medigap insurance — called Medicare SELECT — was scheduled for introduction in 15 states: Alabama, Arizona, California, Florida, Indiana, Kentucky, Michigan, Minnesota, Missouri, North Dakota, Ohio, Oregon,

Texas, Washington, and Wisconsin. If you live in one of these states, ask your state insurance department about the Medicare SELECT policies that have been approved for sale there.

The difference between Medicare SELECT and standard Medigap insurance is that Medicare beneficiaries who buy a Medicare SELECT policy will be charged a lower premium in return for agreeing to use the services of certain designated health care professionals.

These health care professionals, called "preferred providers," will be selected by the insurers. All insurers, including some HMOs, will offer Medicare SELECT in the same way standard Medigap insurance is offered. The policies are required to meet certain federal standards and are regulated by the states in which they are approved.

Action You Should Take

To keep up with the continuing changes in Medigap insurance, and be fully informed of all its provisions, you are advised to take these easy actions:

Call **1-800-772-1213**, the toll-free number of the Social Security Administration, which is responsible for providing information about Medicare and for handling enrollment. Ask for a free copy of *The Medicare Handbook*. You can call on any business day from 7 a.m. to 7 p.m.

Also, please help yourself — and other Medicare seniors — by reporting any insurance agent who claims to be an "official" representative of the Medicare program. It is a federal offense for any private insurance agent to claim that he or she represents the Medicare program in trying to sell you an insurance policy. The federal toll-free number for reporting your complaint is: 1-800-638-6833.

Your copy of *The Medicare Handbook* should answer all your questions about Medigap insurance. But let us add just one final word of advice: never, *never* buy more than one Medigap insurance policy — you can never collect on more than one.

22

Support Groups: What's the Magic?

Come along with us to a typical meeting and see for yourself how a support group works.

This one is called "Better Breathers." It is sponsored by a local hospital, will meet once a month in a spacious room the hospital rents in a regional mall, and follows guidelines from the American Lung Association. There is no charge for participation in the group.

Eighteen women and six men show up for the season's first meeting. They had read about it in the newspaper. They are all retirees and they start exchanging first names as they take places in a circle of chairs. The atmosphere is relaxingly informal. There are fruit juices and cookies on a table, and one woman has brought her knitting.

The group leader introduces herself. "Just call me Kathy." she says. "I'm a respiratory therapist and I'll do my best to answer all your questions as we go along. But first I'd like to go around the circle and find out why you're here and what your special interests are."

Understanding COPD

The seniors all have one of three chronic obstructive pulmonary diseases (COPD): asthma, bronchitis, and emphysema. Some are taking an occasional sniff from their oxygen inhalers. One man, in a wheelchair, has his portable oxygen tank with him.

Their main interest, they say, is in learning how to master a variety of basic breathing exercises. Kathy assures them they will be practicing breathing exercises for at least 10 minutes at every future meeting.

"Remember," she warns them, "oxygen is a drug; you need a prescription from your doctor to get it. And you have to be very careful how you use it — cranking it up to larger amounts than your doctor recommends could reduce your stimulus to breathe."

There are some informal, volunteered comments about individual practices. One man says, "I'm on oxygen during sleeping hours only," and he adds a few comments about that. One woman says, "When I cut off the oxygen, I can barely make it from the bedroom to the living room. I keep my nebulizer machine in the living room, instead of the bedroom, because it's noisy; it wakes up my husband. During the night, I just use my inhaler."

Within 15 minutes, there's a free and lively sharing of personal experiences. Each person's comments seem to trigger questions and comments from others. Kathy gently keeps the discussion on track and on time.

Some Favorite Topics
There are exchanges of current, first-hand information about the best sources of inhalers and other needs at the lowest prices; about changes in Medicare allowances; about trustworthy and slow-pay Medigap insurance companies; and about the costs of home health care. One woman complains, "My husband's bill for oxygen is now up to three hundred dollars a month. Anybody have any ideas about how to cut it down?"

By the end of the first hour, most of the participants have exchanged phone numbers, and there are some after-meeting huddles on such topics as best restaurants for a smoke-free environment; some stores to be avoided because of the dusty remodeling; and worst places in the state for pollen. In a support group, there seems to be at least one well-informed researcher on almost any question that comes up.

One woman asks Kathy if the time period can be extended from one hour to an hour and a half. Kathy says she will bring it up for a vote at the next meeting.

A man tells Kathy that he used to be a heavy smoker and asks what percentage of the people in a group like this one are here because of smoking. Kathy reflects for a moment. "Usually," she says, "about eighty percent were smokers."

One month later, the opening of the second session is like a reunion of old friends. "It's nice," says the woman with the knitting, "to be with people who understand where I'm coming from. I used to feel all alone most of the time, like some kind of freak."

Better Ways to Breathe
"Today," Kathy tells the group, "you're going to start learning two new ways to breathe more efficiently. The first is *pursed lips* breathing and the second is *diaphragm* breathing."

In pursed lips breathing, she explains, we inhale through the nose; then we purse our lips slightly, as if to whistle, and exhale slowly — but not forcefully — through pursed lips.

"Pursing your lips slows down the breathing rate," says Kathy. "It also creates a little back-pressure in the lungs — enough to keep the airways open longer."

Diaphragm breathing comes in for a longer explanation, and we all make notes about an exercise we need to do later, when we can lie on the floor.

Kathy opens the discussion of diaphragm breathing with a surprise. "Most of you have probably grown up thinking that the best way to breathe was to *throw out your chest*. Right? *Wrong.* I want you to learn that the most important muscle in breathing is your *diaphragm*. It does — or should do — about sixty-five percent of the work of breathing. So, instead of throwing out your chest, practice pushing out your abdomen, right below your rib cage."

Basic Exercises

When we get home, Kathy wants us to do this: "Lie on your back with your knees bent. Place a book on your abdomen, just below the rib cage. Now, while you're keeping your upper chest as still as possible, inhale through your nose and push the book upward with your abdomen. Watching the book rise is the proof that you're using the diaphragm right. Next, exhale slowly — through pursed lips — and watch the book move downward. And all this while, don't use any muscles in your chest, your neck, and your shoulders."

Kathy warns us that the diaphragm breathing exercise will seem strenuous at first — "because most of you have been using what we call the 'accessory muscles' in your neck, shoulders, and chest, instead of the diaphragm muscle. So your diaphragm muscle went flat and your lungs lost their elasticity. You need to build up and strengthen your diaphragm muscle — the stronger the muscle, the less energy, and oxygen, you'll need for your breathing. Try to do that exercise for five minutes at a time, four times a day."

Walking, she tells us, is good exercise for people with COPD. "And always inhale through your nose for two counts and then exhale slowly, through pursed lips, for four counts." Other good exercises are riding a stationary bike and lifting light weights.

"Always do the hardest part of any job while breathing out," she says. "Remember to do that when you're lifting, pushing or pulling, walking uphill, or climbing stairs.

"And always stop," Kathy warns us, "whenever you feel pain — any pain means you're going too far. We'll get into more of that at our next session. See you back here in a month!"

Other Support Groups

The "Better Breathers" meet in a shopping mall. Other support groups meet in church social halls, mental health centers, hospital lounges, savings-and-loan community rooms, firehouses, and private homes. Support groups come in all types and sizes — some as affiliates of established, national organizations, others as purely local groups. Ask your local hospital or mental health center about the groups now operating in your area. If a support group does not exist for your particular problem, your local hospital or mental health center can show you how to start your own group.

For a handy listing of support groups of special interest to retirees — and usually operating in most areas — please refer to Chapter 4, "The Resources Around You."

Support groups are now forming an important echelon of America's healthcare system. During his term as Surgeon General of the U.S. Public Health Service, Dr. C. Everett Koop convened a special Workshop on Self-Help and Public Health, in 1987, and stressed these key points: "I believe in self-help as an effective way of dealing with problems, hardship, and pain. ... Mending people, curing them, is no longer enough; it is only part of the total health care that most people require."

How the Groups Began

It is generally agreed that Alcoholics Anonymous, born in Akron, Ohio, in 1935, was the principal prototype of what we now call support groups. A.A. came into being in an almost accidental way when a desperate alcoholic, on the verge of another binge, had a sudden hunch that, if he could find another suffering alcoholic to help, he might in turn save himself.

Bill Wilson, a 40-year-old Wall Street securities dealer, had come to Akron on a business venture that collapsed, leaving him in deep despair and almost penniless. His frantic calls from a public phone booth in a strange city, in search of another alcoholic, ultimately led him, in a roundabout way, to Henrietta Seiberling, member of a distinguished tire-manufacturing family and a highly respected scholar in the field of prayer. Henrietta Seiberling thought immediately of Dr. Bob Smith, a 55-year-old Akron surgeon, for whose sobriety she had been praying.

Weeks earlier, Bill Wilson's New York physician, a specialist in the alcoholism field, had told him: "You have an obsession of the mind that compels you to drink, and an allergy of the body that condemns you to go mad or die." Now, in his Akron moment of blind fear, Bill Wilson had a sudden conviction that his wild hunch about helping another alcoholic might indeed be his last hope.

Henrietta Seiberling told him she thought prayer, too, might help. In her prayers for Dr. Bob, a daily drinker, she said she had received a clear spiritual warning that he could not just cut down on his drinking — he would have to abstain totally. "It's the first drink," she said, "that's starting all the trouble. He *must* not pick up that first drink."

Dr. Bob's wife, Anne, got involved later in the discussions and said there was some ancient support for Bill Wilson's hunch about helping a fellow sufferer. She opened her Bible to the Book of James and quoted: "Faith without works is dead."

There was early agreement that any lasting relief from any affliction that affected both the mind and the body would have to come from "some power greater than ourselves." But it took four more years of experimental work with other alcoholics to put together a combination of elements that seemed to deliver consistent, predictable results.

The A.A. Report

In 1939, Bill Wilson and Dr. Bob Smith published a booksize report on their work. They had intended to call the book *A Way Out* — but then a movie with that title appeared, so they switched their book's title to *Alcoholics Anonymous* for the simple reason that, for privacy's sake, they had withheld the real names of all the persons mentioned in the book. Alcohol addiction, in 1935, was generally regarded not as a disease but as a moral weakness, and no self-respecting person wanted to be identified with it.

The Wilson-Smith book carried a description of a 12-step spiritual philosophy that was designed to create significant attitude change; and a comprehensive report on the treatment and recovery of typical participants in the experimental program encompassing some 100 alcoholics. Wilson and Smith claimed a recovery rate of 75 percent.

The report was an immediate sensation because physicians who specialized in alcohol problems tended to agree that "most of the people in that program were beyond the reach of other remedial measures."

The success of the book also brought a prompt change of the name of the founding group from *The Alcoholic Foundation* to *Alcoholics Anonymous*.

Isolating the Secret

Scientific researchers began at once to sort out the commonplace parts of the A.A. program, looking for the "magic ingredient" that made it so effective in healing people who had an affliction that was both psychological and physiological — people who previously had often been given up as hopeless.

Dr. William D. Silkworth, Physician-in-Chief at New York's Towns Hospital, was the eminent specialist who had given Bill Wilson the dire prognosis of madness or death. Dr. Silkworth, who would treat some 40,000 alcoholics during his lifetime, had also mentioned the chance of help from "some sort of spiritual experience," but only as a remote possibility. In the A.A. program, the dedicated doctor quickly focused on two simple elements that impressed him as having unique value.

The first element was the instant rapport that seemed to materialize between any two people who suffered from the same disease. One alcoholic, Dr. Silkworth noted, enjoyed greater trust from another alcoholic than would be given to any outsider, even a doctor. This basic trust was leading to a surprisingly faithful carrying out of instructions.

The second simple-but-unique element was the fact of being surrounded by a fellowship of people who understood the sufferer's problem and offered a dimension of mutual encouragement: "the person no longer feels alone."

Helper Therapy

Dr. Harry M. Tiebout, one of America's most respected psychiatrists of the day, reported to the American Psychiatric Association, in 1943, that "the central therapeutic force is spirituality," but went on to single out one other element for special praise.

"Helping others," Dr. Tiebout told his colleagues, "is a two-way situation, since it not only assists the beginner in his first efforts, but also aids the helper, who derives from his efforts something which is essential for his own continued well-being."

Dr. Silkworth's comments about rapport, trust, and mutual encouragement — together with Dr. Tiebout's recognition of "helper therapy" as a new approach to healing — soon attracted followers in other healthcare fields. The original A.A. concept, complete with its spiritual philosophy, was soon adopted by groups of people suffering from other forms of addiction disease, and later by most chemical dependency treatment centers. Followers with mostly-physical problems disregarded the spiritual philosophy, but made good use of rapport and mutual encouragement in dealing with complex, little-understood afflictions, such as Alzheimer's Disease.

Some groups adopted the "anonymous" from the A.A. name; others did not. A.A. chooses, for some interesting reasons other than public opinion, to continue being "anonymous."

Visiting the Groups

With or without the "anonymous" label, most support groups welcome visitors who have a sincere interest in the subjects being discussed. Your local hospitals and mental health center can steer you to almost any group that might be of some current or future help to you or to someone you care about. Just ask. Visitors to an Alzheimer's support group, for example, can learn more from a few hours of listening to the first-hand caregivers than they could learn from days of reading.

If your locality does not have a support group for the problem that concerns you, ask your hospitals or mental health center about starting a group that would be a local affiliate of a national organization — or ask about starting your own, independent support group. The healthcare professionals can guide you, at no charge, and the community events editor of your local newspaper can give you the publicity you need to attract early joiners.

23

Eating Right

$\boldsymbol{T}$he 1990s opened a whole new chapter of nutrition guidelines for retirees. Some highlights:

- In 1992, the U.S. Department of Agriculture announced its revolutionary new Food Guide Pyramid and Dietary Guidelines, designed to shift a nation to low-fat, low-calorie, high-fiber foods, with five-a-day servings of fruits and vegetables.

- In 1993, the Nutrition Screening Initiative introduced a massive program aimed at identifying and treating malnourishment among senior citizens.

- Also in 1993, the U.S. Food and Drug Administration (FDA) completed an overhauling of food labels so that, for the first time, all food packages, including meats, are required to show how much fat, saturated fat, cholesterol, dietary fiber, and sodium they contain — information of special interest to persons concerned about heart disease and cancer.

- Weight loss, always a major problem among older people because of bodily changes due to aging, was helped by new findings.

- Eating out, a favorite retiree pastime, made new health gains as low-fat, low-cholesterol, and low-calorie selections were added to restaurant menus.

The Food Guide Pyramid

In the USDA's new Food Guide Pyramid, shown on the following page, we see the familiar four food groups we've grown up with: the whole grains (now called the "bread group"), the vegetables and fruits, the dairy products (now called the "milk group"), and the meat/fish/poultry group (now called the "meat group"). So what's new?

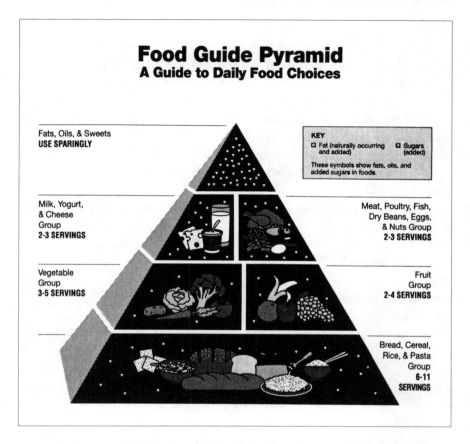

Food Guide Pyramid
A Guide to Daily Food Choices

Fats, Oils, & Sweets
USE SPARINGLY

KEY
□ Fat (naturally occurring   □ Sugars
and added)   (added)

These symbols show fats, oils, and added sugars in foods.

Milk, Yogurt, & Cheese Group
2-3 SERVINGS

Meat, Poultry, Fish, Dry Beans, Eggs, & Nuts Group
2-3 SERVINGS

Vegetable Group
3-5 SERVINGS

Fruit Group
2-4 SERVINGS

Bread, Cereal, Rice, & Pasta Group
6-11 SERVINGS

What's new is that Fats, Oils, and Sweets are confined to the slim tip of the pyramid, and that Fruits and Vegetables are now being recommended on a five-servings-a-day basis (compared with our earlier average of about three and one-half servings per day). The details are all spelled out in the seven guidelines.

The Dietary Guidelines

1. Eat a variety of foods to get the energy, protein, vitamins, and fiber you need for good health.

2. Maintain healthy weight to reduce your chances of having high blood pressure, heart disease, a stroke, certain cancers, and the most common kind of diabetes.

3. Choose a diet low in fat, saturated fat, and cholesterol to reduce your risk of heart attack and certain types of cancer. Because fat contains over twice the calories of an equal amount of carbohydrates or protein, a diet low in fat can help you maintain a healthy weight.

4. Choose a diet with plenty of vegetables, fruits, and grain products which provide needed vitamins, minerals, fiber, and complex carbohydrates, and can help you lower your intake of fat.

5. Use sugars only in moderation. A diet with lots of sugars has too many calories and too few nutrients for most people and can contribute to tooth decay.

6. Use salt and sodium only in moderation to help reduce your risk of high blood pressure.

7. If you drink alcoholic beverages, do so in moderation. Alcoholic beverages supply calories, but little or no nutrients. Drinking alcohol is also the cause of many health problems and accidents and can lead to addiction.

Explanatory Notes

Fats in foods are mixtures of three types of fatty acids — saturated, monounsaturated, and polyunsaturated. *Saturated* fats are present in largest amounts in fats from meat and dairy products and in such vegetable fats as coconut, palm, and palm kernel oils. *Monounsaturated* fats are present mainly in olive, peanut, and canola oils. *Polyunsaturated* fats are present mainly in safflower, sunflower, corn, soybean, and cottonseed oils, and in some fish.

Of these three types of fat, *saturated* fat is the one to worry about. Eating too much saturated fat raises blood cholesterol levels in many people and increases their risk for heart disease. The Dietary Guidelines recommend limiting saturated fat to about one-third of total fat intake.

Cholesterol and fat are not the same thing. Cholesterol is a soft, waxy substance that is present in all parts of the body. Our bodies produce cholesterol, and we get additional amounts from animal foods — meat, poultry, fish, milk and milk products, and egg yolks. High blood cholesterol is one of the three major risk factors for coronary heart disease— cigarette smoking and high blood pressure are the other two.

Our cholesterol level is determined partly by our genetic makeup and partly by the saturated fat and cholesterol in the foods we eat. Even if we didn't eat any cholesterol, our body would manufacture enough for our needs.

Cholesterol becomes a threat when it builds up in the walls of the

arteries that supply blood to the heart. Do you know what your blood cholesterol level is? Please find out from your doctor — who will also explain
that, along with this "bad" cholesterol, there is also a "good" cholesterol.

The Food Pyramid and Dietary Guidelines of 1992 were soon followed
by a national *Nutrition Screening Initiative*, a program that calls for doctors and other health care workers to routinely test older people by 1995
to identify and treat malnourishment.

Nutrition Screening Initiative
The Nutrition Screening Initiative is a cooperative project of the American Academy of Family Physicians, The American Dietetic Association,
and the National Council on the Aging, and is funded in part by a grant
from Ross Laboratories, a Division of Abbott Laboratories. With their
permission, we are reprinting their nutritional health self-test opposite.

The New Food Labels
We have been accustomed, since the mid-1950s, to seeing labels on food
packages that showed us long, detailed lists of ingredients and nutrients
— and surveys confirm that more than 70 percent of grocery shoppers
read those labels before their first-time purchases of a product. One of
the surveys showed that some 20 percent of women and 34 percent of
men definitely changed their minds about a product after reading the
label. If they worried about fat, for example, it was easy to compare Brand
A with Brand B and choose the one with fewer grams of fat.

Those labels, however, were *not* trying to make products more com-
petitive; their purpose was only to keep us informed about essential information.

Beginning with the new generation of food labels — scheduled to
appear during 1993 and possibly into 1994 — the Food and Drug Administration, and the Department of Agriculture (which regulates meat
and poultry products) are going a step further. In addition to present-
ing essential information, they are trying to promote *healthier diets*. For
example, the labels give specific information about the amounts of fat,
saturated fat, cholesterol, dietary fiber, and sodium in a product, because
that information can be important to consumers who want to reduce their
risk of heart disease and cancer.

Vitamins A and C stay on the labels because they offer some protection against cancer, anemia, and osteoporosis. But the B-vitamins (which

The Warning Signs of poor nutritional health are often overlooked. Use this checklist to find out if you or someone you know is at nutritional risk.

DETERMINE YOUR NUTRITIONAL HEALTH

Read the statements below. Circle the number in the yes column for those that apply to you or someone you know. For each yes answer, score the number in the box. Total your nutritional score.

	YES
I have an illness or condition that made me change the kind and/or amount of food I eat.	2
I eat fewer than 2 meals per day.	3
I eat few fruits or vegetables, or milk products.	2
I have 3 or more drinks of beer, liquor or wine almost every day.	2
I have tooth or mouth problems that make it hard for me to eat.	2
I don't always have enough money to buy the food I need.	4
I eat alone most of the time.	1
I take 3 or more different prescribed or over-the-counter drugs a day.	1
Without wanting to, I have lost or gained 10 pounds in the last 6 months.	2
I am not always physically able to shop, cook and/or feed myself.	2
TOTAL	

Total Your Nutritional Score. If it's —

0-2 **Good!** Recheck your nutritional score in 6 months.

3-5 **You are at moderate nutritional risk.** See what can be done to improve your eating habits and lifestyle. Your office on aging, senior nutrition program, senior citizens center or health department can help. Recheck your nutritional score in 3 months.

6 or more **You are at high nutritional risk.** Bring this checklist the next time you see your doctor, dietitian or other qualified health or social service professional. Talk with them about any problems you may have. Ask for help to improve your nutritional health.

These materials developed and distributed by the Nutrition Screening Initiative, a project of:

 AMERICAN ACADEMY OF FAMILY PHYSICIANS

 THE AMERICAN DIETETIC ASSOCIATION

 NATIONAL COUNCIL ON THE AGING, INC.

Remember that warning signs suggest risk, but do not represent diagnosis of any condition. Turn the page to learn more about the Warning Signs of poor nutritional health.

will continue to be in the foods) have been dropped from the labels because they are no longer considered essential information.

The key element in the new labels is the column of numbers under the heading *Percent of Daily Value*. Those numbers show you how much of a day's ideal total you're getting of any particular ingredient.

The "ideal total" is based on a daily diet of 2,000 calories. Large, active people need, of course, to adjust the calories upward; small people with a sedentary life-style need to adjust the calories downward.

Weight Control

Many retirees are not aware that, although physical activity and body processes tend to slow down with age, the body's need for most nutrients continues unchanged. Thus, to get such essential nutrients as proteins and carbohydrates, vitamins and minerals — without gaining excess weight — a senior needs to hold down the daily intake of calories (the heat-producing or energy-producing value in food when oxidized in the body).

Seniors are advised: learn your "healthy weight" and eat only enough calories to maintain that weight.

And what is your "healthy weight"? There is no exact answer. The genes that run in your family influenced your body type and weight. And, as people age, their natural body weight and distribution of fat tend to change. Recent research suggests that people can add a little weight as they grow older without added risk to health.

The height and weight table shown will help you decide whether or not your weight is healthy. The table, derived from the National Research Council, carries ranges of weights because of individual differences in muscle and bone.

There are risks in being too fat or too thin. Being too fat is a common problem in America and it carries the risk of high blood pressure, heart disease, stroke, the most common type of diabetes, certain cancers, and other illnesses. Being too thin is less common, but it often is linked with osteoporosis in

Suggested Weights for Adults

Height[1]	Weight in pounds[2] 35 years and over
5' 0"	108-138
5' 1"	111-143
5' 2"	115-148
5' 3"	119-152
5' 4"	122-157
5' 5"	126-162
5' 6"	130-167
5' 7"	134-172
5' 8"	138-178
5' 9"	142-183
5' 10"	146-188
5' 11"	151-194
6' 0"	155-199
6' 1"	159-205
6' 2"	164-210
6' 3"	168-216
6' 4"	173-222
6' 5"	177-228
6' 6"	182-234

[1] Without shoes   [2] Without clothes

The higher weights in the ranges generally apply to men, who tend to have more muscle and bone; the lower weights more often apply to woman, who have less muscle and bone

Source: Derived form National Research Council
(From a booklet published by USDA and HHS)

women and shorter life expectancy in both women and men.

Researchers also agree that, for adults, body shape is important to health. Excess fat in the abdomen is considered a greater health risk than excess fat in the hips and thighs. The U.S. Department of Health and Human Services offers these suggestions for checking your body shape:

- Measure around your waist near your navel while you stand relaxed, not pulling in your stomach.

- Measure around your hips, over the buttocks, where they are largest.

- Divide the waist measure by the hip measure to get your waist-to-hip ratio. If the ratio is close to or above *one*, you may want to talk to your doctor about your weight.

Avoid Crash Diets

The Food and Drug Administration (FDA) warns consumers against quick-fix claims for weight-loss diets, pointing out that only as few as 5 percent of the dieters will keep the weight off in the long run. The FDA has banned 111 ingredients once found in over-the-counter diet products. None of those substances, which included alcohol, caffeine, dextrose, and guar gum, proved effective in weight-loss or appetite suppression. Some pills, such as amphetamines, are highly addictive and can have an adverse effect on the heart and central nervous system.

To lose weight safely, we are advised: either reduce the number of calories we eat, or increase the number of calories we burn off through exercise, or — ideally — do both. The experts also advise: if you want to lose weight, set a goal of about a pound a week. A reduction of 500 calories per day will meet that goal because a total reduction of 3,500 calories is required to lose one pound of fat.

To make your dieting easier, the experts offer these tips:

- Choose from a greater variety of foods and eat smaller portions.

- Load up on foods naturally high in fiber: fruits, vegetables, legumes, and whole grains.

- Limit portions of foods high in fat: cakes and pastries; red meat; dairy products like cheese, butter, and whole milk.

- Exercise at least three times a week.

Eating Out

When retirees were asked, in one national survey, to name their favorite activity, "eating out" was topped only by reading in all its forms.

Eating out carries the great health benefit of socializing; but it also carries some nutrition risks because, on average, more than half of our meals away from home are at fast-food restaurants where fried chicken and fried fish can be as high in fat and calories as a high-fat hamburger.

For all your eating out — whether it's at fast-food or conventional restaurants — the nutritionists offer these guides to healthier habits:

- Avoid fried foods; choose broiled, baked, or grilled meats and fish, and baked or mashed potatoes. Avoid chips, nachos, and croissants.

- Salad dressings can be loaded with calories; get them on the side and use them lightly, or ask for oil and vinegar — or skip the dressing entirely.

- Sauces: marinara (tomato) sauce is better for you than white sauces. Guacamole is high in fat. So is sour cream.

- Desserts: either cut them out or cut down.

- Portions: if the restaurant serves large portions, eat only half and take the rest home in a doggy bag.

Do You Need Vitamins?

Vitamin and mineral supplements are strongly promoted; but most nutritionists worry about the over-use of such products. If our daily diet is varied and well-balanced, they say, we should be getting all the vitamins and minerals we need. Their advice is always: *ask your doctor.*

The nutritionists point out that B and C vitamins are *water*-soluble, so that excessive amounts are flushed away and your only problem is wasted money. A and D vitamins, on the other hand, are *fat*-soluble, so that very high quantities can be detrimental and can even lead to cases of toxicity. The nutritionists also ask us to remember that protein supplements can be dangerous for persons with impaired liver or kidney function. Again: ask your doctor.

Water and Laxatives

One top nutritionist makes this special plea to all retirees: "Please remember that *water* is an essential element in your diet. Drink eight to ten glasses of water or other liquid — coffee, tea, milk, or soups — every day. Many of the older people are forgetting to do this.

"Water is essential to your *regularity*. Constipation is turning many seniors to laxatives — which can lead to additional problems because laxatives flush away vitamins and nutrients that didn't have time to be absorbed by your body. It gets to be a vicious cycle."

Learning More

Every week, usually on Thursday, most daily newspapers carry special articles on food. And all the while, your county's Cooperative Extension Service home economists offer free publications and periodic seminars — covering the world of nutrition, shopping, menu-planning, and food preparation. You may wish to ask your Cooperative Extension Service to put you on a free mailing list.

Cookbooks

We asked a group of professional dietitians in hospitals and county health departments to name their choice of cookbooks for retirees who are concerned about their nutrition. Here are the recommendations of those dietitians:

The American Heart Association Cookbook, 3rd edition 1979, David McKay Company, Inc., New York, NY, Ballantine Books Division of Random House, New York, NY.

The American Heart Association Low-Fat, Low-Cholesterol Cookbook, Grundy, S., 1989, Times Books, NY.

Weight Watchers Cookbooks, published by Weight Watchers.

Count Out Cholesterol, Ulene, A., 1989, A. Knopf, Inc., NY.

Controlling Cholesterol, Cooper, K., 1988, Bantam Books, NY.

Low Cholesterol Cuisine, Lindsay, A., 1989, Hearst Books, NY.

The Fat and Sodium Control Cookbook, Dayne, A. and Callahan, D., Little, Brown and Co., Boston.

The Low Salt, Low Cholesterol Cookbook, Waldo, Myra, G.P. Putnam's Sons, NY.

24

Getting More (and Easier) Exercise per Hour

The fitness professionals offer you an easy-to-take prescription for feeling good again — and feeling good about yourself. The prescription has two simple ingredients:

- Every day, put a leisurely hour into moderate exercise.

- Three times a week, do 20 minutes of aerobic exercise.

Moderate exercise can be a mixture of stretching and suppling exercises, calisthenics, yard work, lifting light weights, and easy walking — all activities that build muscle and improve flexibility.

Aerobic exercise can be rapid walking, jogging, bicycling, swimming — all activities that improve heart and lung action.

It sounds so easy, you may want to charge right into it today and make up for lost time. But the pros advise a slower approach.

E-a-s-e into It

Before we start *any* exercise program, we're told to get a complete medical checkup. Next, we should start with a twice-a-week workout of less than 10 minutes, easing up to a workout of about 20 minutes three or four times a week. If any of this activity leaves us feeling tired the next day, the rule is: reduce the workout time temporarily and then increase it gradually.

We're also advised, on a continuing basis, to start each day with a lazy stretching and suppling program. As little as 10 minutes a day of stretching can help to relax and rejuvenate our muscles. Here, opposite are some examples of good stretching exercises.

After the morning stretch, the experts recommend *walking* as the simplest, most natural way to begin any exercise program. If you think that sounds too simple, think again. Walking is no longer just a dull left-right-left. Walking, according to some of the professionals, is "the only exercise you'll ever need."

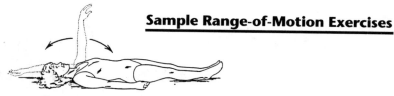

Sample Range-of-Motion Exercises

Figure 1. Shoulder.
Lie on your back. Raise one arm over your head, keeping your elbow straight. Keep your arms close to your ear. Return your arm slowly to your side. Repeat with your other arm.

Figure 2. Hip
Lie on your back with your legs straight and about six inches apart. Point your toes up. Slide one leg out to the side and return. Try to keep your toes pointing up. Repeat with your other leg.

Figure 3. Knee and Hip
Lie on your back with one knee bent and the other as straight as possible. Bend the knee of the straight leg and bring it toward the chest. Push the leg into the air and then lower it to the floor. Repeat, using the other leg.

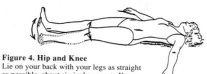

Figure 4. Hip and Knee
Lie on your back with your legs as straight as possible, about six inches apart. Keep your toes pointed up. Roll your hips and knees in and out, keeping your knees straight.
  To further strengthen knees, while lying with both legs out straight, attempt to push one knee down against the floor. Tighten the muscle on the front of the thigh. Hold this tightening for a slow count of five. Relax. Repeat with the other knee.

Figure 5. Shoulders
a) Place your hands behind your head.
b) Move your elbows back as far as you can. As you move your elbows back, move your head back. Return to starting position and repeat.

Figure 6. Thumb
Open your hand with your fingers straight. Reach your thumb across your palm until it touches the base of the little finger.

Figure 7. Knee
Sit in a chair high enough so that you can swing your leg. Keep your thigh on the chair and straighten out your knee. Hold a few seconds. Then bend your knee back as far as possible. Repeat with the other knee.

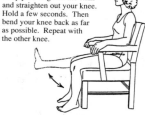

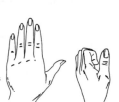

Figure 8. Ankle
While sitting a) lift your toes as high as possible. Then, return your toes to the floor and b) lift the heels up as high as possible. Repeat.

Figure 9. Fingers
Open your hand, with fingers straight. Bend all the finger joints except the knuckles. Touch the top of the palm. Open and repeat.

Courtesy of Florida Hospital/Waterman

Walking's Good News

Our wellness centers are now promising: "A regular walking program can help you lose weight, tone flabby muscles, and have more energy. It can help prevent heart disease, relieve the pain of angina, and avoid mental depression. Walking is rhythmic, involves half of the body's 650 muscles and 208 bones, and is continuous. Many doctors prescribe walking for their heart patients because it's good for cardiac fitness."

Walking lets you choose your own speed, from a "stroller" rate of 20 minutes per mile (3 mph) to a "brisk" walker rate of 15 minutes per mile (4 mph) to an "aerobic" walker rate of 12 minutes per mile (5 mph). Along with helping your heart and your muscles, you will be burning calories at the rate of about 100 calories per mile.

Because walking involves the use of so many muscles, we are cautioned to begin with a period of warming up and stretching, before we leave our house, to avoid pulling or tearing a cold muscle.

Warming Up and Stretching

Take several minutes to loosen up and elevate your heartbeat with a low-impact movement like walking in place. Set a deliberate pace, lifting the knees slightly.

After warming up, do a series of gentle stretches, holding each stretch for 20-30 seconds with no bouncing, in this sequence:

Arms: Stand with your arms extended to the sides at shoulder level. Holding your arms out straight, draw large circles in the air, relax, then reverse direction.

Calf and Achilles tendon: Stand an arm's length from a wall and put your palms against the wall. Keeping your body straight, lean forward, letting your elbows bend to develop the stretch down the calf and Achilles tendon. Hold.

Quadriceps: Stand on your left leg, balancing yourself with your right hand on a chair or a wall. Hold your right foot in your left hand behind you and pull gently towards the buttocks. Hold, then repeat with the other leg.

Hamstring: While standing, cross your feet, placing them parallel a few inches apart. Bend from the waist very deliberately, hands clasped lightly, arms hanging loosely. Bring your head close to your knees without straining. Hold. Recross your legs and repeat.

Groin: Sit up straight on the floor, the soles of your feet together, knees dropped towards the floor. Place your hands on your toes, your elbows on the inside of your knees, and gently lean forward, bending from the hips. Hold.

The Way to Walk

Walk slowly at first, breathing easily, arms swinging freely from the shoulders. Find a regular, comfortable rhythm. Stand tall but relaxed, your head level, shoulders back, rib cage lifted, stomach pulled in to support the torso, pelvis forward, and your weight set over your hips.

When you feel warmed up, move out in a brisk stride, planting your heel at a 45-degree angle, locking your ankle, and rolling forward smoothly. Stretch your hips forward and have the weight-bearing leg straight by the time your hips pass over it into the next stride. Your arms should swing freely, brushing your sides, elbows bent at a 90-degree angle, hands closed in a loose fist.

Don't bob; move fluidly with a slight feeling of "leaning in" to your stride. Breathe evenly from the abdomen, inhaling through the nose for two steps, then exhaling from the mouth every two or three or four steps, whichever is more comfortable.

A simple but accurate way to see if you are walking at a good aerobic pace is to walk as briskly as you can while maintaining a comfortable conversation with a partner.

As the conclusion to your walking workout, always return to a slow pace to cool down, and then finish the cool-down with some gentle stretching.

Choosing Your Shoes

Sooner or later, along with your conscientious attention to warm-ups and stretches and cool-downs, you're sure to start thinking of treating your feet to a good pair of shoes made especially for walking.

The crafters of good shoes like to point out that your two feet have 52 bones (one-fourth of the body's total), 64 muscles and tendons, 218 ligaments, eight arches, and just over 50 miles of blood vessels and nerves. When we walk at a brisk pace, our feet bear nearly one-third more weight than when we are standing still. Good walking shoes are designed to help our feet roll along in a smooth, heel-toe motion, with more flexible soles for faster walking.

Along with beveled toes and heels for proper toe-off and heel-plant, and a molded rearfoot construction for extra stability, the finest walking shoes have a water-filled insole. The water in the insole flows back and forth under the foot with each step, providing the wearer with the sensation of a continuous foot massage.

To keep track of your mileage, you'll want a pedometer, and you might opt for a pair of hand weights for toning your upper arm and shoulder muscles while you walk. Hand weights have proved to be virtually useless as calorie-burners, but at least they needn't interfere with your swinging stride. Ankle weights, on the other hand, can unbalance your limbs and hyperextend your knees.

As one more accessory for your walking, you might like a good map of your area. When walking in your own neighborhood begins to seem boring, try starting your walk in other areas within an easy drive. Do some exploring; discover new places of interest.

When the weather is bad, of course, most of us avoid extremes in heat and cold by simply walking in our nearby air-conditioned mall. The main entrance opens for walkers at 6 a.m., we have the spacious corridors to ourselves, we meet new walking friends, and we enjoy some browsing in stores that open early — including the ones that sell athletic equipment.

Muscle-Resistant Machines

Some of our older retiree friends depend on us to keep them informed about new products, so we watch the store displays and read the ads. We have been pleasantly surprised by the low prices on such muscle-building equipment as the stationary bicycle, rowing machine, side-rail skier, treadmill, and weight bench. The prices are hard to resist.

On the other hand, our nearby wellness centers have a complete choice of muscle-resistant machines — plus a swimming pool — and health care professionals on hand to give us careful supervision.

Aquacize

Swimming pools, in recent years, have been doubling more and more as aquacize centers. As all of us grow older, and begin to learn about arthritis and osteoporosis, we also are discovering the shockproof, weightless world of aquacize. In a heated pool, we can build strength and flexibility in our muscles and joints without the pain of doing it on land. We can walk, jump, and learn special, therapeutic exercises. Aquacize is now as close as your nearest wellness center, with physical therapists to supervise your individual program.

Dancing and Yoga

Senior Centers everywhere offer a choice of dance activity, from square dancing to round dancing to ballroom dancing. The exercise is moderate and it offers the great bonus of socializing, meeting new friends.

Yoga, which has been revered in faraway places for more than 5,000 years, is only now being discovered by many American retirees. Yoga involves breathing techniques, stretching exercises, balancing movements, the holding of positions, and meditation. Yoga may look gracefully slow and effortless, but a woman in leotards — or a man in sweats — can be damp with perspiration within half an hour.

Teachers of yoga like to point out that it goes beyond physical conditioning and becomes a highly practical kind of stress management — it helps people work toward what is called the "relaxation response," a physiological state characterized by relaxed muscles, lowered blood pressure, and a feeling of tranquility.

"Body Recall"

In the something-for-everybody world of senior fitness programs, one of the most imaginative is "Body Recall," a physical conditioning procedure for adults who have lost muscle tone and flexibility. "Body Recall," which requires nothing but a straight-backed chair and an electrical outlet, was developed at Kentucky's unique Berea College by Dorothy C. Chrisman, a fitness professional, and has since been honored by the U.S. Public Health Service's Office of Disease Prevention and Health Promotion as an "Exemplary Contribution to Healthy Aging." Body Recall exercises are executed slowly, with no jerking or jumping, while sitting in the chair, and while holding the back of the chair for balance as the exerciser goes through other movements.

Learning More

- Ask about the variety of exercise programs available now at your senior centers, wellness centers, YMCAs, and local health clubs.

- Ask your librarians and booksellers about the wide selection of popular books on physical fitness.

• Look on the newsstands for magazines devoted to walking, running, bicycling, swimming, golf, tennis, and many other activities — including some you may never have heard of.

• For information about Body Recall, write: Body Recall, Box 412, Berea, KY 40403.

25

Sexuality Comes of Age

The year 1992 was survey time for the subject of sex among retirees, and the news media had a field day. In their invasion of bedroom privacy, the pollsters focused on the percentages of each age group who were still "doing it" and the frequency with which the doing-it was being done — and in what odd ways. The reports made spicy reading. But beyond all the titillating trivia, there was a vast lack of helpful information.

Said one disgusted professional in the marital-counseling field: "It's kind of an Olympics mentality. Why do we have to apply numbers to sex? Won't all this just be discouraging to couples who aren't keeping up with the record breakers?"

Happily, for all of us who treat our intimate times with grateful respect and would like to enhance them if we can, a professional husband-wife team had already written "the definitive book" about sex in retirement before the surveys struck. And now the authors have updated the book with significant new information.

The authors: Dr. Robert N. Butler and his wife, Myrna I. Lewis. Dr. Butler, a Pulitzer Prize-winning author and former director of the National Institute on Aging, is Chairman of the Department of Geriatrics and Adult Development of Mount Sinai Medical Center in New York. Myrna I. Lewis, a psychotherapist specializing in the social and health issues of mid-life and older women, is a member of the faculty of the Mount Sinai School of Medicine.

The book: *Love & Sex After 60.* The first edition of this landmark book, published in 1976, brought a strong demand for continuing, updated editions. The latest edition, published by Ballantine Books, appeared in 1993.

The authors have granted us permission to give you a sampling of the highlights of a book that is both comprehensive and concise.

Defining "Sexuality"

"Sexuality," Butler and Lewis tell us, "goes beyond the sex urge and the sex act. For many older people, it offers the opportunity to express not only passion but affection, esteem, and loyalty. It provides affirmative evidence that one can count on one's body and its functioning. It allows people to assert themselves. It carries with it the possibility of excitement and romance. It expresses delight in being alive. It offers a continuous challenge to grow and change in new directions."

Along with conceding that many retired couples have lost interest in sexuality, the authors offer many revealing insights into why the condition exists, and how it can be corrected.

About Women

After a reassuring explanation of the sexual changes in women associated with the menopause ("a rich source of folklore"), and the modern treatment of those conditions, Butler and Lewis point out that "the predominant pressure on women comes from what can be termed *aesthetic narrowness*, that widespread assumption that only the young are beautiful. Many older women believe this themselves."

In practical terms, the book notes: "Women in good health who were able to have orgasms in their younger years can continue to have orgasms until very late in life, well into their eighties. Indeed, some women begin to have orgasms for the first time as they grow older."

About Men

"Men are special victims," say Butler and Lewis, "of a lifelong, excessive emphasis on physical performance. Masculinity is equated with physical prowess. Older men judge themselves and are judged by comparing the frequency and potency of their sexual performance with that of younger men. These comparisons seldom place any value on experience and the quality of sex."

Because of all the *macho influence*, the authors continue, "Most men begin to worry secretly about sexual aging some time in their thirties." Ultimately, men worry about impotence, defined as "the temporary or permanent incapacity to have an erection sufficient to carry out the sexual act."

Most sex therapists, Butler and Lewis report, "do not consider impotence or erectile dysfunction to be a problem unless it occurs in 25 percent or more of sexual encounters with the same partner." Moreover: "many cases — perhaps the majority — can be improved or reversed with proper diagnosis and treatment."

The authors note bluntly that "an older man ordinarily takes longer to obtain an erection than a younger man. The difference is a matter of minutes after sexual stimulation rather than a few seconds."

They also note that men past 50 produce less semen than younger men and add: "This can be a decided advantage in love-making since it means that the older man can delay ejaculation more easily and thus make love longer, extending his own enjoyment and enhancing the possibility of orgasm for his partner."

Butler and Lewis conclude: "In general, men do not lose their capacity to have erections and ejaculations as they age. The patterns of sexual activity of healthy men as they grow older tend to reflect the patterns earlier in their lives, with the added factor of a somewhat slower physical response due to aging. Problems that occur, particularly impotence, are caused by physical or psychological difficulties and are frequently treatable."

In complete, easily-understood terms, the book offers a comprehensive background on all the principal medical problems associated with sex, and how they are treated today.

About Couples

As a guide to couples, Butler and Lewis tell us: "Physical stimulation, at first involving the body as a whole and later focusing on the genitals, is an important part of arousal. Masters and Johnson initiated a three-stage method of 'sensate focus,' which is now used by many sex therapists to teach people to relax and slowly move each other into a state of sexual arousal, eventually resulting in sexual climax. The stages are, first, a stepwise nongenital 'pleasuring,' of one's partner's body by touching and caressing; second, genital touching and caressing without intercourse; and third, nondemanding sexual intercourse where the goal is pleasure rather than performance.

The book covers special techniques to stop or slow premature ejaculation by men, and adds: "The majority of women receive their primary sexual satisfaction from clitoral stimulation, and that direct or indirect clitoral stimulation is the initial requirement in the production of female orgasm."

In its extensive coverage of changes due to aging, the book reports that changes in and around the clitoris are slight and concludes: "it still remains the source of intense sensation and orgasm, essentially as it was in earlier years."

About Offspring

Butler and Lewis explain in helpful detail why the attitudes of grown sons and daughters can inhibit the sexuality of their parents: "Many adults continue to be bound by a primitive childhood need to deny their parents a sex life and to lock them into purely parental roles. For these children, their parents are never fellow adults.

"Nor are the motivations always psychological," the authors continue. "Avarice and selfishness are, unhappily, common. If one parent dies, children may try to prevent the surviving parent from meeting new friends (and potential new partners) in order to protect their inheritance."

About Other Problems

With eminent professional authority, the authors discuss the full range of sexual concerns among retirees, including emotional and social-conditioning problems; guidance for persons with cardiac pacemakers or who have had heart attacks or coronary bypass surgery; the occasional importance of self-stimulation (masturbation); homosexual relations; widowhood, dating, and remarriage; and where to go for professional help on special problems.

Sexuality is treated, throughout the Butler-Lewis book, with professional objectivity and great sensitivity. In our opinion, and that of our close friends, *Love & Sex After 60* deserves a place on your bookshelf, and a continuing sharing of its helpful information with other retirees you care about.

26

Getting Your Sleep

*F*ew mysteries in all recorded history have generated as much curiosity and speculation as the semi-conscious state we call *sleep*. The ancient Greeks prayed for guidance from Morpheus, their god of dreams. Psychologists and physiologists came later, probing the changes that take place in our brains and bodies during the approximately one-third of our lives we spend in bed. But not until recent years did scientific sleep disorders centers report their biggest breakthrough findings about sleep — especially among retirees.

- In 1990, the National Institutes of Health reported that half of all people aged 65 and older experience sleep disturbances of one kind or another, with insomnia — trouble falling asleep or staying asleep — as the most common problem.

- Also, in 1990, the American Sleep Disorders Association, the major national organization in the sleep research field, dispelled the myth that "older people need less sleep." As we grow older, the experts agreed, we simply get less of the deeper stages of sleep and we awaken more often. Example: young adults usually awaken briefly about five times during the night; but people in their 60s and older often awaken as many as 150 times a night.

- Researchers have now discovered the causes of more than 80 different disorders of sleeping and waking. Most of the causes are fairly easy for any layperson to understand. Two principal offenders are panic and pills.

What Is "Normal" Sleep?

To get a briefing on sleep disorders and how they are treated, we visited the sleep disorders center at a leading hospital and talked with a professional polysomnographer. Her "office" was like a hotel's executive suite, with a pleasant sleeping room adjoining a room loaded with technical apparatus.

"The first thing I tell people about sleep," Luanne Witzofsky said, "is that it's not just 'light' or 'deep.' It goes in *cycles* — usually four or five separate cycles each night — and each cycle has a number of distinct *stages*. The main stages are drifting off. Then Delta, the deepest sleep. Then REM — which means 'rapid eye movement' — sleep."

People who walk around in their sleep, she explained, are in the deep Delta stage. But REM sleep is probably the most fascinating stage. In REM sleep, the eyes move from side to side, back and forth, with such regularity that the movement can be monitored with instruments and recorded. Early in the night, the REM stage may be limited to a scant 10 minutes. Later, it may last for 30 to 40 minutes. It's during the REM stage that we usually do our dreaming.

We raised a hand. "And what," we asked, "is a normal night's sleep? What's the ideal number of hours?"

"The ideal number," said Luanne, "is whatever you want it to be for *you*. If you get up fresh and rested, wanting to charge into your day, you've had the right number of hours. Don't worry about hours unless you just can't seem to function well the next day." Luanne paused and looked at a card.

Our Body Clock

"I've told you about cycles and stages," Luanne continued. "Now let me mention that our body runs on what's called a circadian rhythm, like a body clock. The circadian rhythm makes our sleeping more complicated because it's a twenty-*five* hour interval, not twenty-*four*. If we lived in caves, in total darkness, our body clock would advance an extra hour every day, and we would tend to go to bed one hour later, and get up one hour later, during every twenty-four hour period. If you've ever had jet lag, after flying nonstop through two or more time zones, you know how uncomfortable it can be to have to re-set your body clock."

Luanne showed us some paragraphs she had marked in technical reports from the Harvard Medical School and the Stanford Medical School. "The subject of sleep," she said, "can be very technical at times, but you won't have any trouble understanding it. We've been talking about insomnia — having trouble falling asleep or staying asleep. That's the most common of all the sleep disorders and sometimes it will be caused by a complex of two or more things. But a case of insomnia often boils down to one or two simple causes — panic or pills. Panic and pills tend to go together."

How Panic Works

If we've seen any television commercials for sleep aid pills, Luanne said, we'll understand how easily panic can take over in a person who is trying vainly to sleep. The scenario usually goes like this:

We see a person in bed, tossing and turning in dramatic fashion. He or she suddenly sits bolt upright and looks at a clock. The camera zooms in for a close-up of the clock face. It shows a late hour. Now we see a close-up of the face of the anguished sleeper as he or she exclaims, "I've just got to be ready for that meeting in the morning. It could make or break my whole career. *I've just got to get some sleep!"*

We hear a musical sting, then see another close-up of the clock. Another full hour has passed. In obvious desperation, the tormented insomniac lunges out of bed and heads for a bottle of sleep aid pills. We see an extreme close-up of the brand name on the bottle as the pills are washed down with a glass of water. A super appears on the screen, in small type: "For occasional relief as directed." Then we see the person drifting happily off to sleep. The smile says volumes.

"When people get panicky," Luanne explained, "the harder they try, the worse it all gets. Then, if they start popping pills, everything gets even worse."

Read the Labels

Television viewers seldom read more than the small super, "For occasional relief as directed." If they are careful enough to read the warning label on the package, they could see a message like this:

"Do not take this product if you have asthma, glaucoma, emphysema, chronic pulmonary disease, shortness of breath, difficulty in breathing, or difficulty in urinating due to enlargement of the prostate gland unless directed by a physician. Avoid alcoholic beverages while taking this product. Do not take this product if you are taking sedatives or tranquilizers without first consulting your physician. If sleeplessness persists continuously for more than two weeks, consult your physician. Insomnia may be a symptom of a serious underlying medical illness."

One of Luanne's booklets from the authoritative American Sleep

Disorders Association carried the warning: "The over-use of both pre-scription drugs and over-the-counter medications to aid sleep in older people worries physicians and other health professionals. While people over age 65 constitute about 13 percent of the American population, they consume more than 30 percent of prescription drugs and 40 percent of all sleeping pills. Yet recent studies show that some commonly used drugs may not work well in older people or may even make their sleep prob-lems worse."

Good Sleep Habits

Instead of turning to pills for a quick fix, the American Sleep Disorders Association recommends these guidelines:

- Get up at about the same time every day, regardless of when you go to bed. Recent research suggests that lingering in bed a short while in the morning eases the transition between sleep and waking and improves alertness in older people.

- Organize your day. Regular times for eating meals, taking medicines, performing chores and other activities help keep our inner clocks running smoothly. Spend time outdoors, particularly in the after-noon, when weather permits; recent studies suggest that regular exposure to bright light also helps synchronize our body clocks. People with certain types of sleep and mood disorders may benefit from use of artificial lights several times brighter than ordinary room lights. A sleep specialist will tell you if this treatment is appropriate for you.

- Keep active. Exercise regularly, and as vigorously as you can, in the late afternoon. Two or three hours before bedtime, take a walk or do some simple stretching.

- If you nap, try to nap at the same time each day. Mid-afternoon is best for most people.

- Avoid caffeine within six hours of bedtime. Don't drink alcohol or smoke at bedtime.

- Use alcohol sparingly, especially when sleepy. Even a small dose of alcohol will have a much more potent effect when you are sleepy.

- Go to bed only when sleepy. Establish relaxing presleep rituals, such as a warm bath, light bedtime snack, or watching the news on TV.

- If you are a bedtime "worrier," dedicate another time — say 30 minutes after supper — to writing down both problems and possible solutions.

- Reserve your bed for sleep and sex only. Don't, for example, use your bed or bedroom as an office or place to watch TV.

- If you can't sleep, don't stay in bed fretting. After 10 or 15 minutes, go to another room and read or watch TV until you feel sleepy.

- Try spending less time in bed. If your doctor has determined that no physical disorder plays a role in your insomnia, consider sleep restriction. This new anti-insomnia treatment is based on the finding that many insomniacs spend excessive amounts of time in bed, hoping to make up for lost sleep.

- Use sleeping pills conservatively. Most doctors seldom prescribe them for use every night or for longer than three weeks. Current recommendations call for taking a sleeping pill for a night or two, then skipping a night or two or longer if you sleep better. Don't take a sleeping pill after drinking alcohol.

When to See a Doctor

The experts advise: If your sleep has been disturbed for more than a month and interferes with the way you feel or function during the day, see your family doctor or internist or ask your doctor to refer you to a sleep disorders specialist.

If your doctor sends you to the sleep disorders center we visited, they probably will begin by asking you a long list of evaluation questions — some of which can be answered more accurately by your bed partner, or other members of your household — than by you. Here are a few sample questions:

1. "If you are awakened during the night, is it hard for you to get back to sleep?"

2. "You may not be aware of it, but have you been told that you snore loudly?"

3. "Even after you slept well the night before, do you sometimes feel sleepy — or actually fall asleep — even when you're driving a car?"

4. "Do your legs sometimes twitch or jerk suddenly during the night? Do you need at times to get up and walk around, or move your legs in some way?"

To professional polysomnographers like Luanne Witzofsky and her colleagues, question No.1 points to insomnia — trouble falling asleep or staying asleep— and insomnia comes in three types. Mildest is *transient* insomnia, triggered by excitement or stress — enough to cause several nights of poor sleep. Next comes *short-term* insomnia — resulting in several weeks of poor sleep — also caused by stress, the serious stress of a divorce, serious illness, or death. Finally, we have *chronic* insomnia, a complex disorder with many possible causes, that disturbs sleep every night, or most nights, or several nights a month. One in three American adults is currently losing sleep over one of these types of insomnia, but help is now close at hand.

Sleep Apnea

Question No.2, concerning snoring, suggests possible sleep apnea. (Apnea, a Greek word, means "want of breath.") And whereas up to 30 percent of all adults snore, with no serious medical consequences, snorers with the obstructed airways of sleep apnea should do something about their problem. Sleep apnea, most commonly found among overweight, middle-aged men, can be treated with something as simple as tennis balls sewn in a pajama top — or with a beeping "position monitor" — to keep the snorer from lying on his or her back. More serious cases, in which a person stops breathing during sleep for as long as a minute — and does it hundreds of times during the night — usually call for a weight-loss exercise program, and perhaps for the use of a respironics device that delivers a small amount of pressure, applied through a mask over the nose, to prevent structures in the throat from blocking air movement in and out of the lungs. The device is so quiet it won't disturb a bed partner, is lightweight and portable for travel, and has a DC power capability for camping and boating.

Narcolepsy

Question No.3, concerning sudden drop-offs to sleep, is a clue to narcolepsy. One of our good friends once discovered his narcolepsy by dropping off to sleep on a California freeway, at the top allowed speed. Fortunately, he struck no other cars and walked unscathed from his own after it rolled over three times. Narcolepsy, which often is genetic, can be treated with stimulants.

"Restless Legs"

Question No.4, concerning leg movements, relates to a disorder known variously as *periodic limb movements* (PLM) and as *Nocturnal Myoclonus*. PLM seldom awakens the sleeper fully, but can become highly memorable for the bed partner who is being kicked throughout the night. Many people with PLM also experience "restless legs" when awake, a crawling sensation in the calves or thighs when they are sitting or lying down. PLM responds well to a variety of medications.

Bad News/Good News

Lack of awareness of common sleep disorders has led to some very sad conditions among retired people. An estimated two-thirds of all the people living in long-term care facilities have sleep disorders of one kind or another — which too often are simply treated with tranquilizing drugs. The drugs, in turn, can lead to further confusion and a greater risk of falls. On the good-news side, today's 80-some sleep disorders are now well understood, and trained sleep technicians like Luanne Witzofsky — following doctors' orders — can monitor and record your body movements, breathing, and heart and brain activity while you sleep obliviously through an overnight polysomnogram.

For more information on sleep disorders, our readers are invited to write to the National Sleep Foundation, 122 South Robertson Blvd., Suite 201, Los Angeles, CA 90048, for a free copy of *Sleep As We Grow Older.*

27

Keeping Your Memory Up

New York educator and activist Florence Hunter, at 69, became bored with retirement and decided to run for a state-level political office; but then came the panic of wondering how her over-age memory would handle the mass of strange new faces and names.

Roger Manning of Chicago, who had planned to spend the rest of his life on the fairways, suddenly missed the excitement of media sales; but doubted that he could ever cope again with all the mass of names and numbers.

Cliff and Donita Paine agreed it would be stimulating and convenient to move into the retirement village in Western Michigan; but it was intimidating to face a whole new circle of people they had never met before.

They were all worried enough to go hunting for wise guidance, either from healthcare professionals or from understanding friends, and were promptly advised: "Don't *worry* about it! You're letting your worry turn a natural kind of self-concern into a *problem*."

Some Calming Facts

- Retirees tend to worry needlessly about Alzheimer's Disease. Only about 2 percent of the people between 65 and 75 will develop it.

- Most of what you are now "forgetful" about is fading in a natural, wholesome way because it is no longer important to your functioning. You're just cleaning your mental attic.

- Memory power, like everything else about your health, is subject to the bottom-line rule that applies to all human organs: "What you don't use, you lose." Memory, like muscles, needs exercise.

- The most common cause of what most retirees call "memory loss" is usually rooted somewhere in apathy, poor nutrition, neglected hearing or vision, or (very commonly) in the over-usage of alcohol or other drugs, both prescription and over-the-counter.

One doctor advised our friends: "Always remember that a person with a true senility problem, like Alzheimer's, is seldom *aware* of the problem. It's normal, as we get older, to do more forgetting of such trivial details as where we left our sun glasses." But he also advised: "A healthy memory is something you can't just take for granted. You have to work at it. How? For openers, try brushing up on some old habits your parents tried so hard to teach you."

The Old "Tidy Habits"

Keep an orderly mind as well as an orderly room — don't clutter it with junk. Be selective about what goes into your mental memory bank. Learn to review and discard old information to make way for new, more useful information.

Finish what you start — one task at a time. Don't deliberately confuse yourself by trying to do two or more things at the same time.

If it's important, write it down. Memory experts discovered long ago that we remember, over any given period of time, about 10 percent of what we *hear,* about 50 percent of what we *read,* and about 90 percent of what we *do.* Keep a little, fail-safe notebook in your pocket or purse and *write things down.* Review your notes every night and transfer what's important to another good source.

One of the memory experts our friends consulted had just computerized his office. "Look," he said, "we're all living in what's called the information age-' We're being taught how to *access* basic information sources in easier, faster ways. You retirees can access information very effectively with the simplest kind of memory aids.

Handy Memory Aids

Classify essential information — legal, financial, medical, product manuals and warranties, family/friends — put it in well-marked files or loose-leaf binders, and keep it in a file drawer or on a shelf within easy reach. You never have to feel any anxiety about not knowing an item of information as long as you know exactly where you can find it.

Buy a wall calendar with spaces for at-a-glance reminders of appointments, trips, special bills to be paid, important birthdays and anniversaries, and other events you want to be sure to remember.

Use information stickers in your car (about service needs), your utility room (more service needs), your gardening shed (planting and feeding, and spraying schedules), over your work desk (things to do today), and on the refrigerator door (more things to do today). This is all "robot information," so don't burden your brain with it. Save your brain for better things.

Medication: count out the day's pills each morning and store them in a compartmented container. Also, ask your pharmacist about the innovative new medication reminder devices now on the market.

Before starting trips, short or long, make a card listing the routes and stops and clip it to your car's sun visor.

The wall calendar and other memory aids were a big help to Florence, Roger, Cliff, and Donita — but only up to a point. What they still needed, for remembering names and faces — especially in stressful, large-group situations — was some memory *improvement*, not just aids. What was needed, one advisor said, was a disciplined, three-step approach they could practice and master.

Memory Improvers

1. Pay close attention to the people you meet, trying earnestly to form clear pictures of their special characteristics — always looking for one or two dominant, unique features — while at the same time repeating their names at least once, and asking about the derivation of unusual names. "Your mind is a camera," the advisor had said. "You need to focus it sharply on what you want to register."

2. Add dimension to that mental picture by writing the name down later, and by learning more about those people and then *visualizing* them in their career fields (teacher, homemaker, merchant) and in their favorite leisure activity (art, golf, foreign travel). When recalled, they would then "come alive."

"What we're talking about here," the advisor explained, is *mnemonics* — various devices for helping you remember things. Mnemonics (NEE-MONICS) is a simple and very old science that began with the ancient

Greek philosophers — Plato, Aristotle, Simonides. It's based mostly on what we call 'association of ideas.' For example, a unique nose, or hair style, or height will help you remember a person who has any feature like that. Mnemonics is nothing new to you — you used mnemonics in childhood when you learned simple rhymes like 'thirty days has September, April, June, and November.'

"It takes some practice," the advisor warned. "Improving memory power is like improving muscle power — you have to work at it. And you have to do it for yourself."

3. Don't pass the buck to other people in your memory improvement program. The advisor (who was speaking to Roger Manning) said sternly: "You have a wife, Helen, who watches over you like a guardian angel. She is always ready to remind you of all the things you're supposed to remember for yourself. If you turn that responsibility over to Helen, you are making her what we call an *enabler* — and that's not fair. The responsibility for your memory improvement is *yours*."

Inevitably, one of our friends asked: "But what if I do all that and can't see any improvement? What if I — or some one close to me — can see a definite decline in my memory?"

"In any case like that," the advisor said, "I would tell you: don't worry, don't panic — just talk it over with your doctor. He may want to check out some simple possibilities in diet or medication, or a vitamin deficiency, or the harmful interaction of some prescription drugs. Or he may suggest further testing by a specialist.

"Reliable memory tests have been around for years, with no stigma attached. So please don't try any self-diagnosis. Check with your doctor. Or, if you don't have a favorite doctor, check with your local mental health center, or your hospital. Above all, don't start jumping to any wild conclusions about something you're just guessing about."

Learning More

Your library and your bookseller have a choice of books about protecting and improving your memory. Look them over. Try, of course, not to discourage yourself by reading books that promise overnight miracles. Be realistic.

28

Ask Your Pharmacist

Among America's health symbols, one of the best-known and most trusted is the white-coated pharmacist. Asking for professional guidance on drugs from the neighborhood pharmacist has always been a friendly custom.

Now it's a law. Since January 1, 1993, all pharmacists have been *required* to provide counseling services, "at least to Medicaid patients," on all matters the pharmacist regards as "significant." The definition of "significant" under the federal law (OBRA-90) covers special directions and precautions about side effects, interactions, proper storage, techniques for self-monitoring, and other essential guidance. The federal legislation, which must be implemented by all states receiving Medicaid funds, has now become a national invitation to all consumers to step right up to the pharmacy counter and ask about anything they don't fully understand.

The federal and state action was prompted, in large part, by concern about the well-being of senior citizens. According to the National Institute on Aging, about 25 percent of all seniors take four to six drugs concurrently, often prescribed by different doctors. The chances for confusion are obvious.

What Customers Ask About

According to the pharmacists we interviewed in key retirement areas, the most frequent questions from their senior customers are these:

Side effects. "I'm on a prescription drug for *(condition)*. Is it safe to take this over-the-counter drug *(shows package)* at the same time?"

"I have prescriptions here from two different doctors. Is it safe to take both of these drugs at the same time?"

"I'm taking this prescription *(shows bottle with label)*. Do I have to be careful about what I eat, or what I drink, while I'm taking this?"

"Is it safe to drive when I'm taking *(name of drug)*?"

Purpose of drug. "I have this prescription (*shows it*), but I've forgotten what the doctor said about it. Can you tell me what this is for?"

Vitamins. "For my osteoporosis, should I be getting natural vitamins or the ones with chemical additives?"

Aspirin. "You've got all kinds of aspirin. What kind am I supposed to take for a blood thinner?"

Laxatives. "Should I be taking this bulk laxative or one of the other kinds?"

Eye drops. "I have glaucoma. What kind of eye drops should I use for dry, itching eyes?"

Aches and sprains. "What's good for a bad back?"

Storage. "How long can I keep this medicine, and how should I store it?"

Don't Forget Generics

Along with your questions about side effects and other safety considerations, always ask if there is now a generic substitute for your prescription drug — and if it is appropriate. Drug patents run out after 17 years. In as many as 35 cases out of a hundred, your prescription drug is now available as a generic. Buying the generic substitutes can often save you 30 percent or more. But always ask your pharmacist about the reliability of the generic brand.

More ways to save. Because prescription drug prices have been soaring for more than a decade, a tragic number of seniors can no longer afford to buy the prescription drugs they are told to take. If you share that problem, be aware of three ways to ease it: 1) Always ask your doctor for some of the free samples all doctors receive from the drug companies as promotional materials; you are entitled to them, on a trial basis, to see if they help your condition. 2) Ask your doctor about the no-charge plans many ethical pharmaceutical makers have for patients with limited funds. 3) Always call several pharmacies for price quotations before you buy a prescription drug. Prices often vary dramatically.

More ways to be safe. Please note the additional comments about drugs in the chapter entitled, "What's Ahead in Senior Health Care?"

29

What You May Not Know about Drug Addiction

By the time they reach retirement age, most people have listened to all the lectures they ever want to hear about the possible problems of America's beloved drug, alcohol.

A neighbor of ours recently told his daughter, in a sudden burst of anger: "Look, I'm sixty-nine years old. Any drinking I do is my own damned business and nobody else's!"

The seniors say they've heard all they ever need to hear about the chances of being impaired by intoxication, addiction, and heart or liver damage. And they've warned their daughters about alcohol-related birth defects.

But the seniors seem to know little or nothing about the drug phenomenon that should be of the very highest interest to every retiree: the synergistic interaction of alcohol with other drugs.

Synergistic Interactions

Your dictionary defines *syn-er-gism* as "cooperative action of discrete agencies such that the total effect is greater than the sum of the total effects taken independently." In simpler terms: synergism involves a multiplier factor so that 2 + 2 = 5 (or more).

The innocent mixing of alcohol with other drugs became a national, page-one story on June 11, 1985, when a New Jersey schoolgirl, Karen Ann Quinlan, died after a 10-year coma induced by having a few alcoholic drinks after taking some tranquilizer pills. The coma was finally ended, after a court battle, when her parents were granted permission to have the life supports disconnected.

A friend of ours learned about synergistic interactions when she was stopped for drunken driving after what she protested had been "only a couple of drinks." She was telling the truth. Then the police officer asked about tranquilizers. "Yes," our friend recalled, "I probably took two for a bad case of nerves." The officer explained that two drinks and two pills were not the same as four drinks or four pills. Rather, he explained, it could be the same as 16 drinks or 16 pills.

Another friend of ours learned about synergistic interactions in an even more dramatic fashion. After quieting his nerves one afternoon with a generous helping of tranquilizers, he continued his self-prescribed relaxation therapy with a rewarding pitcher of martinis. Suddenly, he was startled out of his pleasant reverie by the appearance of a strange beast in his driveway. As he turned in his chair, he had seen the weird creature very clearly through the picture window.

He reacted with the instinct of an old combat veteran. He made a dash for his deer rifle, loaded it, flung open the door, and pumped five fast rounds through the grille of his new Buick. (True story.) The police said later, "He wasn't just intoxicated — he was *crazed*."

How Serious Can It Be?

Our New Jersey friend, Professor Vincent Groupé, is one of America's top authorities on drug addiction. After retiring as a professor of health sciences at Rutgers University, he was called by the National Institutes of Health to serve extensively as a consultant on drug addiction and related problems. On the subject of synergistic interactions of alcohol with other drugs, he says simply, "The multiplier factor usually runs from two to four, but can be higher, and it can be fatal."

Dr. Groupé then ticks off some of the familiar drugs that can spell trouble if mixed with alcohol. Here are some examples:

Painkillers. The simplest over-the-counter painkillers, like aspirin, when mixed with alcohol, become stronger irritants and can cause bleeding in the stomach and intestines, and possible liver damage. Prescription painkillers, like Codeine and Demerol, when mixed with alcohol, can affect the central nervous system in ways that can lead to a loss of effective breathing and death.

Sleep-Aids. Over-the-counter sleep-aids, like Sominex, when mixed with alcohol, can become potent enough to depress the central nervous system. Prescription sleep-aids, like Nembutal, Phenobarbital, and Seconal, when mixed with alcohol, can cause breathing failure, coma, and death.

Heart medications. Hypertensive agents, like Aldomet, Apresoline, Capoten, Catapres, Inderal, and Serpasil, when mixed with alcohol, can lower blood pressure to dangerous levels.

Antidepressants. Drugs like Elavil, Pertofrane, Sinequan, Tofranil, and Triavil, when mixed with alcohol, can lower a person's ability to function normally and, in certain combinations, can cause blood pressure crisis.

Tranquilizers. Familiar products like Equanil, Librium, Mellaril, Milltown, Prolixin, Sparine, and Thorazine, when mixed with alcohol, can cause additional depression of central nervous system functions, including severe impairment of such voluntary movements as walking and the use of hands. These combinations can also cause liver damage, respiratory failure, and death.

Other Senior Problems

The National Institute on Aging, and other authorities in the field, regard the mixing of alcohol with other drugs as a special retiree problem for a variety of reasons. One in every four senior citizens is on some form of medication, and half of them are taking more than one medication. To complicate the problem further, persons who once drank socially with impunity can no longer handle alcohol as well as they once did because of natural increases in body fat (which can make an elderly man, as a drinker, the equal of a young lady). Postmenstrual women have an additional problem: the hormone estrogen heightens and prolongs the effects of alcohol.

For all these reasons, the National Institute on Alcohol Abuse and Alcoholism (NIAAA) now recommends that the elderly limit their alcohol intake to one drink a day.

Public health authorities agree that the problem of alcohol is usually underestimated because so many of the older people live alone, drive less, don't need to report for work, and thus keep their problem hidden. Health authorities are deeply aware that alcohol addiction is increasing among retirees because of their loneliness, health problems, and the losses of mates and friends. The National Institute on Aging classifies about one-third of all senior problem drinkers as "late-in-life" drinkers who began their excessive drinking for temporary relief — which led in time to problems.

Alcohol addiction is a terminal disease. Problem drinking, if not treated, usually ends in one of three ways: insanity, a vegetative state, or death by accident or other causes. The House Select Committee on Aging reported in 1992 that 20 percent of all the elderly people now hospitalized in the United States have been diagnosed as alcoholics.

Warning Signs

The National Institute on Aging encourages retirees to help the problem drinkers in their midst by watching for these signs of possible trouble ahead:

- Drinking to calm nerves, forget worries, or reduce depression
- Losing interest in food
- Gulping drinks and drinking too fast
- Lying about drinking habits
- Drinking alone with increased frequency
- Injuring oneself, or someone else, while intoxicated
- Getting drunk often (more than three or four times in the past year)
- Needing to drink increasing amounts of alcohol to get the desired effect
- Frequently acting irritable, resentful, or unreasonable during nondrinking periods
- Experiencing medical, social, or financial problems that are caused by drinking

Getting Help

Professionals in the chemical dependency field have always warned would-be helpers of problem drinkers that the effort can be frustrating because the first and foremost sign of an alcohol problem is *denial*. The problem drinker often refuses to admit even to himself, or herself, that a problem exists. The denial problem can be at its worst among retirees because they tend to resist advice from younger people.

The best way to approach a problem drinker is with an *intervention* session, involving not only family members and close friends but a trusted physician, or clergyman, or a professional from the mental health center or health department. Once the person is persuaded that a problem exists and should be treated, says the National Institute on Aging, "he or she has an unusually good chance for recovery because the seniors tend to stay with treatment programs."

Getting help can then continue with the advice of a family doctor or clergyman; or through a mental health center, specialized treatment center, health department or hospital; or through a self-help support group like Alcoholics Anonymous. Treatment agencies are usually listed in the Yellow Pages of telephone books under "Alcoholism Information & Treatment Centers."

30

Pets Can Help Your Health

We all learned, almost at toddler age, that "a boy's best friend is his dog." Now, at retirement age, we are learning that a pet can be of highly practical value to an older person in at least four very important ways:

1 A pet can mean companionship and unconditional love, something critically needed by many lonely people.

2 A pet with a bark can make a senior feel more secure against crime, and can often be an effective deterrent.

3 A pet, always in need of some attention, can give seniors a psychologically important sense of being needed.

4 And because the pet requires faithful, continuing care, it helps sustain the senior's sense of responsibility for daily chores, including taking better care of himself.

It is estimated that 60 percent of all American households have at least one dog, cat, bird, or other companion pet. Nationally, especially among retirees, cat owners are now outnumbering dog owners. Meanwhile, pets of all kinds in the retirement world are being squeezed by the no-pet clauses in leases and condominium association rules, by the shrinking of roaming room, by leash laws, and by the rising costs of pet care.

Choosing a Pet

Our original way of selecting a pet was to fall instantly in love with a warm and wriggling puppy. Now we are advised to consider exercise space and needs, vaccinations and other veterinary medical requirements, grooming and training costs, boarding costs when we're on trips — and how well the pet will fit into our life-style. It's important to consider all this very carefully, the experts say, because choosing and keeping a pet can be a highly emotional experience. Impulsive actions can come back to haunt us.

Dogs

There are now 124 recognized breeds of dogs, grouped in seven categories: terrier, toy, hound, sporting, nonsporting, working, and herding. These, in turn, have now led to so many mixed-breed combinations that the experts have stopped counting.

Each of these countless dogs has a unique personality, and such other basic considerations as temperament, size, coat and such inherited traits as hyperexcitability or a tendency for barking.

Because of the mind-boggling gamble involved, retirees are advised to buy a grown dog of known character and housebroken habits, and preferably neutered. The animal can be purchased from a breeder, a pet store, a private owner, or an animal shelter.

Private owners are regular advertisers of dogs — often just to find them a loving home. Many fine dogs wind up in animal shelters simply because their owners moved away, or could no longer afford the feeding, or because the dogs show or breeding or racing days were over. Some shelters offer free dog's to retirees as part of a program sponsored by a maker of pet food. Some dogs in shelters, of course, are there because of behavioral problems; so always ask why the animal is there.

Fleas

No comments about dogs, of course, can be complete without a mention of fleas. Fleas. Cats get them, too, but dogs are more likely to be victims because they usually spend more time outdoors than cats do. If you retire to an area with high heat and humidity, the flea problem can be monumental — you could find it necessary to spray your neighbor's lawn for fleas as well as your own. In any case, your first and best authority on fleas is your veterinarian. The Humane Society of the United States also has a word of advice: ultrasonic collars and ultrasonic room devices can stress some animals and do not repel fleas — and never use chemical flea collars.

Dog trainers offer a further caution: never, as a private owner, have anything to do with attack dogs. Too often, attack dogs in amateur hands can maim or even kill. The consequences can be terrifying.

And veterinarians offer this serious reminder: when you buy any pet, it's wise to ask permission to take the animal to a veterinarian for a checkup, and then to bring it back for a refund if the animal has a health problem. The more quickly you check, the less you'll risk becoming emotionally involved.

Cats

Cats have a serious image problem: the homeless, proliferating strays have been killing birds and becoming a general nuisance. Blame part of that problem on Mother Nature for making cats so prolific — they can start bearing before they are one year old, and can continue having large litters several times a year. Blame the rest of the problem on ignorant, careless people who fail to neuter cats that are not being kept for breeding. The most reputable catteries will not give pedigree papers to a buyer until they have proof of neutering. So, little by little, the proliferation problem is being corrected.

Especially among retirees, cats are now becoming the top choice as pets, primarily because they represent easy maintenance. They are neater than dogs; they take better care of themselves; they like to stay indoors rather than outdoors, where they could pick up fleas and communicable diseases; and they don't need to be walked. Beyond that, the cat owners say, cats are playful and can be entertaining — and they dispute any notion that cats are lacking in affection.

The Choice of Cats

"Get a Rag Doll cat," the owners advise, "if you want high affection. Rag Dolls are so fun-loving and tolerant, you might even need to warn your small grandchildren not to play too roughly with them." Rag Dolls come in all colors, with medium-long hair.

Other affectionate breeds are the short-haired Abyssinians and the long-haired Somalians — all with ruddy, brownish hair ticked with darker color. Siamese cats on the other hand, owners tell us, tend to vary in their displays of affection. And Persians, some say, "just like to lounge around looking glamorous — which, of course, is very appealing to people who prefer regal beauty to playful activity."

The mentions of hair length are worth remembering because long hair needs brushing, not only to prevent matting but to protect the self-cleaning cats from swallowing hair balls.

Cats may be less likely than dogs to go outdoors and pick up communicable diseases; but they do need to see the veterinarian for shots. And owners are cautioned not to allow cats near any house plants that could be toxic (because cats like to chew leaves), and never to give a cat any aspirin (because aspirin, so commonly used with dogs, can be fatal to a cat).

131

As was the case with dogs, retirees are advised to acquire their cats full grown, with mature personalities. Also, as was the case with dogs, it's a good idea to read the ads seeking good homes for pets that can't be kept; and to talk with the people at the shelter, along with the breeders and pet shops — and always to have it understood that the animal can be returned if a checkup by the veterinarian finds a health problem.

Playthings for Cats

Hairballs appear again in any discussion of playthings. The familiar stereotype of a cat playing with a ball of yarn can be misleading, because cats get into trouble when they swallow bits of yarn. For the same reason, fake mice with fuzzy covers should be avoided.

One safe and popular plaything is a long, slim, flexible pole (about four feet long), tipped with a long string (four to six feet long), which in turn is tipped with a feather or piece of denim. When the pole is waved slowly back and forth, it gives the cat an imaginary bird to chase.

Most of all, the owners tell us, cats like to climb; it leads them to a happy combination of height and security. One perennial favorite is a catwalk-type shelf along a wall, close to the ceiling, reached by a series of steps. Don't worry about falls; cats have been known to fall from the top ledges of high buildings with no ill effects, because cats have ingenious ways of falling.

Wee Animals

If dogs and cats will be too large for your space, consider rabbits, guinea pigs, hamsters, gerbils, and domestic rats and mice as good alternatives. Many of these wee ones have unique personalities and will respond to an owner's voice.

A lesser known but current contender for small-pet favor is the ferret, a cousin of the weasel and mink. The International Ferret Association points out proudly that the ferret was domesticated by the Egyptians 500 years before the cat. The Association now recognizes 32 different ferret colors, including albinos with pink eyes, albinos with black eyes, and black-eyed whites with a black stripe down the back.

Visit the Pet Shows

Pet fanciers always encourage retirees to visit all the shows that come to town. Dog and cat and other shows offer a helpful, comparative overview of all the popular breeds and thus can be the quickest, surest way to finding the right pet for you. Also, the giveaway literature at the shows can be an easy cram course on much of what you need to know.

One warning: in considering pet animals, the American Veterinary Medical Association warns you never to acquire any wildlife like raccoons, skunks, and chimpanzees. They can be dangerous, says the A.M.V.A., and in most states it is illegal to buy or keep them.

Fish and Reptiles

Multicolored tropical fish can add a touch of beauty and motion to a room, and can be relaxing to watch. Maintaining an aquarium can become a prideful hobby.

In the reptile family, iguanas are popular; but poisonous snakes and other poisonous reptiles should never be kept as pets.

Birds

Many birds not only enjoy being with people, and make cheerful companions, but are especially good pets for persons who are allergic to dogs and cats.

First-time bird owners are advised to avoid expensive varieties, starting instead with finches, canaries, and parakeets. The highly social, trainable members of the parrot family are popular, but can be expensive, and some like to bite.

It's wise, the experts say, to be fully aware in advance of the special needs of many birds — proper foods, social contact, and cages. A bird won't sing or talk if it is malnourished, lonely, or improperly caged.

Other bird fanciers will advise you: if you like birds, but want to avoid all the care and most of the costs, just buy a bird book and put a bird feeder outside your favorite window. Better still, become a naturalist as well as a bird-watcher — buy a good pair of binoculars, join the Audubon Society, and start going along on their fascinating hikes.

Learning More

Along with visiting all the pet shows, your library, and your book store, you are invited to write to the American Veterinary Medical Association for a free, beautifully-illustrated guide to selecting the right pet. Send your request to: American Veterinary Medical Association, 1931 N. Meacham Road, Schaumburg, IL 60173-4360.

31

Saving Your Skin

It's ironic, in this educated age of wellness, that the most prevalent form of cancer is also the simplest one to prevent. It's even more ironic that many of us actually *ask* for it.

Sun-starved retirees are among the worst offenders. Just watch them on the beaches, on the fairways, on the courts, in their boats, and on the fishing piers — all out to get a tan. Why? Because tans are healthy, right?

Wrong! In one of its consumer updates, the Food and Drug Administration quotes a leading dermatologist's warning: "There's no such thing as a safe tan."

The FDA recalls that the myth of the "healthy tan" began in the 1920s, when a famous fashion designer, Coco Chanel, won spectacular publicity for a deep tan she had acquired on a yachting vacation. Almost overnight, a bronzy tan became the symbol of high fashion, social status ... and health. Dermatologists, ever since, have been trying to set the record straight.

"Tan" or "Injury"?

The professionals who are trying to save our skins would like us to switch our terms from "sun tan" to "sun injury," because what we call a *tan* is simply a sign of our body's desperate effort to protect itself against the intense — and, in time, irreparable — burning by the ultraviolet (uv) rays of the sun. The UV rays are especially sinister because we never *see* them — and often don't *feel* them.

The pain is concentrated on the melanocyte cells that lie just under our paper-thin outer layer of skin, our epidermis. The pain causes the melanocytes to produce melanin, a brown pigmentation. The brown pigmentation, which we call a *tan*, is simply nature's way of shading the cells against additional burning. So what we perceive as a sign of health is really a sign of bodily distress.

Continued burning of the cells can lead not only to several forms of skin cancer but to premature aging of the skin.

After we were duped by the "healthy tan" myth, we began to laugh contemptuously at the old, turn-of-the-century photos of ladies wearing sunbonnets and carrying parasols, and of men wearing long pants and long-sleeved shirts in their leisure activities. Laugh no longer. The sunbonnet set was right.

Choosing a Sunscreen

Along with broad-brimmed hats and protective clothing, we need a protective sunscreen on all exposed skin while we're in sunlight — especially between 11 a.m. and 2 p.m., when the UV rays are most intense.

Sunscreens (formerly called "lotions" and "creams") come in two types: physical blockers and chemical absorbers. The *physical blockers*, like zinc oxide and red petroleum, are thick, opaque coatings that simply *reflect and scatter* the harmful UV rays. The *chemical absorbers*, like the salicylates, benzophenones, cinnamates, and Para-aminobenoate (PABA) derivatives, are aromatic compounds that *absorb* the dangerous, high-energy UV waves and then convert the remaining waves into harmless ones.

The sunscreens carry numbers to indicate their "sun protection factor" (SPF). The SPF number simply indicates how much your "natural sunburn protection time" can be multiplied before you risk burning. If, for example, your skin normally becomes slightly pink after 20 minutes in the sun, *without* protection, an SPF of 15 would mean protection for 15 times longer, or 300 minutes (five hours). But don't gamble on this protection claim — always reapply any sunscreen at least every two hours, and always after swimming or perspiring heavily because the sunscreens differ in their degrees of water resistance.

SPF numbers range from 2 to as high as 50. Dermatologists recommend an SPF of 15 or greater for all skin types.

Know Your Skin Type

To help you choose your best sunscreen protection, dermatologists offer you this list of six skin types, ranked in the order of their tendency to sunburn:

Type 1: Very fair, with red or blond hair, and freckles. Always burns, never tans.

Type 2: Usually fair skinned. Burns easily, tans minimally.

Type 3: Sometimes burns, gradually tans.

Type 4: Usually white skin, with medium pigmentation. Minimum burning; always tans.

Type 5: Medium to heavy pigmentation. Very seldom burns; always tans.

Type 6: Black skins as well as others with heavy pigmentation. Never burns, but tans darkly.

If, after all your matching of sunscreens to skin, you still sunburn more severely than normal, you may be experiencing a photo-sensitivity reaction. This reaction is caused by exposing certain drugs or cosmetics to UV light. If you are taking any prescription drugs, ask your doctor or pharmacist about possible aggravating agents. If your problem is drugs or cosmetics, you will need a "broad spectrum" sunscreen.

Know the Danger Signs

The three main types of skin cancer (named for the cells from which the tumors arise) are: basal-cell carcinoma, squamous-cell carcinoma, and malignant melanoma. The deadliest of these, as you have just guessed, is melanoma; but squamous-cell carcinoma is also a killer and is the most common form of skin cancer among black Americans.

In the early stages, these cancers may appear only as discolorations of the skin. So we are advised to pay close attention to any changes in the size, color, shape, or thickness of preexisting moles or other growths. More definite signs are these:

- A mole, birthmark, or beauty mark that changes color, increases in size or thickness, changes in texture, or is irregular in outline.

- A spot or growth that continues to itch, hurt, crust, scab, erode, or bleed.

- An open sore or wound on the skin that does not heal, or persists for more than four weeks, or heals and then reopens.

If you notice any of these signs, see your doctor without delay. At least 90 percent of all skin cancers are said to be curable — if they are detected earlier. Skin cancers can be removed surgically, destroyed by freezing or heat, or treated by x-ray.

Sunglasses

Along with our skin protection, we are all advised to wear one of three types of sunglasses, as classified by the American National Standards Institute:

Cosmetic use. Lightly tinted for wear in mild sunlight, to block at least 70 percent of UVB rays and 20 percent of UVA rays.

General purpose. Medium-dark tinted for most outdoor use, to block at least 95 percent of UVB and at least 60 percent of UVA.

Special purpose. Dark-tinted glasses for intense sunlight, to block at least 99 percent of UVB and 60 percent of UVA. For extra protection, they should have wide frames that wrap around and shield our eyes against light from the side.

The professionals add that polarized glasses are "good for cutting down on glare; but that does not necessarily mean they block out most UV light, nor does the darkness of the lenses mean much about UV blockage." Also: "Sunglasses are marked to indicate type of protection; if not marked, they offer none."

32

Stress, Depression, and Other Mental Health Hazards

"Don't let any of the terms scare you," said the gentle professional at our mental health center. "All of us, at one time or another, have shown signs of having one of the mental disorders because there is no such thing as a completely normal person."

There are now, he explained, some 400 well-defined psychiatric problems, and we will be hearing a lot about them, day after day, because Congress has decreed the 1990s to be the "Decade of the Brain," a decade of accelerated learning about all the mental disorders that trouble one family in every five.

"All of us dream occasionally about winning a lottery and becoming a millionaire — then we collapse in a blue funk when the money goes to a new immigrant who, to us, seems very suspicious." Our counselor pauses. "In that single thought wave, we show signs of being *manic-depressive,* and then of having a *paranoid personality.* If the disappointment about the lottery makes us want to run away from this dreary, friendless world, we're showing signs of *schizophrenia.* All of us, all the time, are constantly weaving from one side to the other of the center line we call *normalcy.*

"So what we in the mental health profession are concerned with is the *degree* of the problem, and *how long it lasts.* We can help you sort things out and find healthy alternatives — but we can't help until you open up and tell us all about it."

Understanding Mental Illness

The broad spectrum of 400-plus mental problems begins with simple *biochemical imbalances* that can be detected in any thorough physical examination and promptly dismissed as a mental problem.

Then we come to *personality disorders* — defined as a "general failure to adjust to socially acceptable norms of behavior" — which can range all the way from disagreeable "eccentricities" to the antisocial personality of someone who seems always to be in some sort of social or legal trouble (including murder). Paranoia — suspecting much of the time that someone else is "out to get us" — is a personality disorder.

Moving along the spectrum, we come to simple *phobias* and *anxieties*. Phobias can include unreasonable fears of certain situations, such as a strong fear of making fools of ourselves in public. Generalized anxiety can involve irritability, jumpiness, sweating, heart pounding — all very uncomfortable, and often frightening. We might regard much of this as just "emotional disturbance," not as a serious mental problem —but we should be aware of this discomfort, and ask about it, because some of the phobias and anxiety disorders can grow into more serious problems.

At the serious end of the spectrum, we meet the three types of major mental illness: schizophrenia, bipolar disorder (manic-depressive illness), and major depression.

"Older people," our counselor said, "don't need to worry much about schizophrenia — that usually manifests itself in younger people. And so does manic-depressive illness.

"As for the phobias and anxiety disorders, they seem to fade as we get older and learn to adjust to them as minor irritations, not life-threatening attacks. But I'll have more to say about the problem of depression which ..."

We interrupted. "You didn't mention *stress*," we said, "and you didn't mention *Alzheimer's Disease*. Everybody complains about stress these days, and Alzheimer's Disease must be the most widely publicized of all the senior diseases."

"All right," he said. "Let's take those two and then go on with the problem of depression.

"Stress," he said, "is just a built-in part of being alive. We ought to be glad we can feel it from time to time. Life without some stress would be dull. But I'll agree that stress can be confusing and troubling to some people until they learn how to handle it. Yes, we can help people develop a better understanding of stress and how to handle it. But first, look through these papers..." We did. Here's a summary:

Stress: Both Sad and Glad

Stress is triggered by changes, large and small, hurtful and happy, in our everyday lives. Some years ago, Doctors Thomas Holmes and Richard Rahe of the University of Washington Medical School studied thousands of cases of people under stress and developed a landmark Social Readjustment Rating Scale that has since been reprinted in many publications.

The top five most stressful events on the Holmes-Rahe scale are all tragic ones: death of a spouse, divorce, marital separation, detention in jail, and death of a close family member. On a scale of zero to 10, death of a spouse would be 10; the other four would be a 7 and three 6s.

But then, as we move down the Holmes-Rahe scale, we find that the joyous event of marriage, a 5, would be on a par with being fired from work. A *promotion* at work — and a *demotion* at work — would each rate a 3. An outstanding personal achievement, at 2.8, would be on a par with in-law troubles. A joyous Christmas, at 1.2, would be on a par with a traffic ticket.

We finished our look at the papers and asked our counselor to continue.

"One very important point in what you've just read," he said, "is that we are all moving through varying degrees of stress at all times, and that stress is a highly personal experience. For example, you've seen a grandfather take his grandson for a thrill ride at an amusement park. The stress of it may leave the grandfather paralyzed with anxiety while his grandson is squealing with delight.

"Now," said our counselor, "since you seem to have a lot of curiosity about stress, let me give you some very simple guides to follow:

Handling Stress

"I just told you that stress was a healthy part of being alive," our counselor reminded us. "So here are some easy ways of making it work for us instead of against us:

"**Say no without explaining.** Any explanation just puts you on the defensive and invites some coaxing.

"**Talk it over with a friend.** Ask for the opinion of a brother, a pastor, any good friend. You'll get the problem off your chest, they will feel complimented to be asked for their opinion — and you will get at least one new perspective on something that will convince you the problem was too trivial to worry about in the first place. Sometimes it can be very helpful to just do a little *ventilating*.

"**Exercise it away.** Remember that your mind and your body work together. When you feel a buildup of pressure from anger, nervousness, and frustration, don't just brood about it. Brooding just makes everything worse. If you can't talk it out with a friend, release the pressure into walking, chopping the ground with a gardening hoe, or "killing the ball" on the court or fairway.

"**Conclude the problem.** For example, when you've had the stress of an argument with somebody, bring the matter to a conclusion, once and for all, in one of these ways: First, dismiss the problem as too trivial to be worth any storage space in your head. Second, call the other person and apologize for the misunderstanding or the display of temper. Third, call the other person and make an appointment for a final discussion of the matter — at which time you will have cooled down and will have some notes to quote from. A final airing of the matter will get it out of your system and let you forget it.

"Whatever you do, don't try to escape from stress by putting some drugs in your system. Drugs can only slow your brain, which makes you less effective — which, in turn, just adds to your stress.

"Now," he continued, "you said you wanted me to comment on Alzheimer's Disease. So let me try to summarize it for you.

Alzheimer's Disease

"We used to use the word *senility* as a blanket term for all memory disorders," our mental health professional said. "Now there's a tendency for people to think of all memory disorders as *Alzheimer's Disease.*

"Before they jump to any hasty conclusions, families who are concerned about Alzheimer's Disease should ask their doctor for a thorough evaluation. The first purpose of an evaluation is to eliminate what we call the '*mimics*' of Alzheimer's. The mimics include nutritional deficiencies, adverse drug reactions, metabolic changes, head injuries, stroke, and depression. By eliminating the '*mimics,*' your doctor's evaluation can often simplify or even solve the problem.

"Are you ready now," he asked, "for my comments about the problem of depression?" We nodded.

Depression

"Depression at any age," said our counselor, "can become a serious mental illness, and it can show up in the older person in a very complex form.

"Depression in the older person can be linked with drugs, or malnutrition, or a lack of social contact. Or it can involve feelings of hopelessness or guilt. Or even thoughts of suicide.

"If the depression begins with the loss of a spouse, it will involve not only grief but the shock of beginning a new life-style — living alone.

"In any case, if the depression in the older person lasts for more than six weeks, it should be regarded as a clinical depression and the family or friends should get professional help for it. Clinical depression affects the total person — not only the person's feelings but his or her behavior, physical health, and the ability to handle everyday decisions. Please tell your friends to take depression very seriously."

As a follow-up to our interview with the counselor at our mental health center, we are adding some notes about another mental health subject most retirees don't like to talk about, but should be aware of. It is a subject of special interest to us because five of our dearest friends have gone that way.

Suicide

Blue Cross reported in 1992 that 1 percent of all Americans over 60 had thought of committing suicide in the past six months. The study was conducted by the Gallup Organization among people living at home, not in care facilities. Loneliness was the most common reason given for considering suicide.

Blue Cross also noted that older Americans "don't talk to their friends about it — they just go out and do it."

Earlier studies of suicide among the elderly have developed this list of warning signs to look for:

- Depression
- Withdrawal
- Loss of appetite or change in eating habits or rapid weight loss
- Loss of interest in activities once enjoyed
- Giving away personal items

Anyone who notices these clues in a loved one or neighbor is urged by the professionals to call a suicide hotline or 911. Suicide clues or mentions should never be ignored or taken lightly.

Learning More

Your mental health center or your hospital can refer you to the professional help you need on any mental health problem. Please do not try to "read up on it" and do your own diagnosing.

Additional background information on Alzheimer's Disease is available from the National Institute on Aging at 1-800-438-4380 (toll free), and from The National Alzheimer's Association's Information and Referral Service at 1-800-272-3900 (toll free).

33

Safety/Security Checklist

Public opinion surveys often suggest that a senior citizen's biggest worry is about crime. The fact is, he or she should worry just as much — or even more — about slips and falls and other accidents. Crime can be traumatic; but so can some of today's medical bills.

Here is a handy checklist to help you start your problem prevention program.

Accident Prevention

❏ **Bathrooms.** Install grab bars in tubs and showers and near toilets. Use non-skid mats, abrasive strips, or carpet on all surfaces that might get wet.

❏ **Bedrooms.** Try to have light switches or night lights — and a phone — within easy reach from your bed.

❏ **Living Rooms.** Avoid having any slippery throw rugs. Keep walkways clear of low tables, footstools, electrical cords. Choose chairs and sofas that are high enough to be easy to get in and out of.

❏ **Kitchen.** Keep all shelves low enough to avoid any need for climbing. If you must climb, use a low ladder, never a chair.

❏ **Garage, cellar, attic.** Keep it clear of anything you could trip over or hit your head or eyes against. Also, keep it clear of inflammable and other hazardous waste.

❏ **Stairs.** Install full-length handrail, and abrasive strips or carpet. Install light switches at both top and bottom.

❏ **Balance.** If you tend to be unsteady, use a cane or walker. If you need to worry about dizzy spells, avoid getting up too quickly after eating or lying down. Also, ask your doctor or pharmacist if any drugs you are taking could affect your balance and coordination.

❏ **Room temperature**. Try not to let it drop below 65 0 F. Prolonged exposure to cold temperatures may cause body temperatures to drop, possibly leading to dizziness.

❏ **Footwear.** Wear supportive, rubber-soled, low-heeled shoes. Avoid wearing only socks or smooth-soled shoes or slippers, especially on waxed or tiled floors. Never walk around at night without slippers to protect your toes.

❏ **Doing yard work.** Wear sturdy footwear with good traction; long pants and long-sleeved shirt; and protective eyewear when using mowers, clippers, other tools. Never work with electric tools under damp conditions. Never fill gasoline tanks while equipment is operating or hot.

❏ **Driving.** Take a refresher course in safe driving at your Senior Center. It can save you on your insurance and it might save your life — or somebody else's. Also, be conscientious about regular vision and hearing checks. And when you are driving, always keep the radio volume low enough to let you hear sirens and other safety signals. Finally: no hitch hikers.

❏ **Boating.** Never operate a boat unless you have taken a basic safety course offered by the U.S. Coast Guard Auxiliary or another boating safety organization.

❏ **Cycling.** Always wear a helmet.

Crime Prevention

❏ **Know your neighbors.** Will your neighbors warn you if they see any suspicious characters around your home? Will you do the same for them? Crime prevention experts put "neighborhood caring" at the top of the crime prevention list.

❏ **Never open a door,** when the doorbell rings, until you know who's there. Make it a habit. Ideally, install a see-through device to let you see who's there.

❑ **Motion-detector flood lights.** Install them on all sides. They turn on automatically when someone approaches.

❑ **Home security system.** Consider buying or leasing a hard wire or wireless security system; but shop around first and compare prices and company reputations. Verify the company's credentials with your local Better Business Bureau.

❑ **Burglar-bar doors.** Caution: do not use burglar bars on windows unless they are hinged and can be opened from inside; fixed bars can trap occupants inside in case of fire.

❑ **Deadbolt locks** and safety chains are a must on all doors leading to the outside.

❑ **Sliding glass doors** should have not only the internal lock at handle but a broomstick or board placed in the track as a second lock.

❑ **Your street number.** Be sure it's easy for the police and fire drivers to see at night.

❑ **Prune shrubs** around windows to remove hiding places.

❑ **Engrave identifying number** on all valuables and ask your law enforcement agency for "ID" window stickers.

❑ **Ladders and tools.** Keep them all locked in your garage.

❑ **Phones.** 1) Remember that cordless phones will not operate in a power failure; you need one conventional phone. 2) For extra speed in calling for help, program your phone for a 911 speed dial. 3) Never answer any personal questions from a stranger over the phone. 4) Never let a stranger into your home to make a phone call; do it for him while he waits outside. 5) Never hesitate to call 911 whenever you see or hear anything threatening or even just suspicious around your home. Law enforcement officers will tell you: "Don't be timid about calling us — that's what we're here for. What counts with us is not the actual danger but only *your perception* of danger."

❑ **Lock cars** whenever they are outside. Always look into a parked car before entering it.

❑ **Apartment buildings**. Use the elevators, not the stairs.

❑ **When you are out,** leave radio and some lights on.

❑ **When on vacation,** ask a neighbor to leave a car in your driveway and pick up any newspapers. Stop mail and newspaper deliveries. Use on-off timers to turn lights on during part of evening. Ask police to put your home on a special watch list.

❑ **Neighborhood Watch Program.** Get involved in one or start one. Exchange phone numbers with neighbors.

❑ **Insurance.** Check your coverage. Many companies now offer reduced rates to customers with approved-type security systems.

❑ **Guns.** Police chiefs advise: "Having a gun just makes you more vulnerable. First, you probably will just lose it to an unarmed prowler who will then have a gun to use against you. Second, most people, especially seniors, cannot bring themselves to kill another human being. Third, shooting somebody can get you into all sorts of legal trouble. Fourth, inquisitive children have ingenious ways of finding guns and creating nightmarish tragedies. Please just call 911 instead."

Fire Safety

❑ **Smoke detectors.** Install them within easy hearing of all rooms (most fires occur at night, when people are sleeping). Test them once a week and replace dead batteries.

❑ **Space heaters.** Keep any heater 36 inches from anything that burns; keep it out of walkways; and turn it off at night before you go to bed. Avoid using electric space heaters in a bathroom or anywhere else around water; or running them off an extension cord that somebody could trip over or be shocked by.

❑ **Fire extinguishers.** Keep them handy, especially near the kitchen, and check their charge regularly.

❑ **Matches and lighters.** Never leave them within reach of children.

❑ **Have an escape plan,** with two escape routes and a specific meeting place outdoors where everybody will meet. In case of fire, always crawl close to the floor in smoke, and feel each door for heat before you open it. If your clothing catches fire at any time, stop, drop to the floor, and roll over and over again to snuff out the flames.

Tornado and Flood Safety

❏ **Follow weather reports.** Know the difference between a watch (when trouble is expected) and a warning (when the trouble is occurring or is imminent). Keep a battery-powered radio in use, with extra batteries on hand.

❏ **Get gasoline for your car.** Gasoline pumps are among the first things that fail in a storm.

❏ **Have window tape, ready to apply.** Flying glass is one of the major dangers in a windstorm.

❏ **Have a safety kit for each family member** at the exit door, comprising a flash light, first aid kit, blanket, extra clothes, and a jug of pure water.

❏ **Know where to go** — your evacuation route and the location of the official shelter or another safe place. In flood water, drive slowly to avoid stalling out your engine.

PERS

PERS is the official abbreviation for Personal Emergency Response Systems, now widely available and in use. The system usually features a small "panic button" on a neck chain, wrist strap, or clipped to one's clothing. When the button is pushed in any emergency, it sends a radio signal to an attachment on your telephone, which automatically dials the emergency response center. The response center calls you back to ask if you need help. If you don't answer within a set number of rings, an ambulance will be sent to your home.

More than 20 different PERS brands are now on the market, and most of them are good values. They can be especially helpful to people with ongoing medical conditions, people recovering from a stroke or other serious problem, and people who are disabled or handicapped.

Unfortunately, the PERS field has been having trouble with a small group of unreliable companies selling inferior products, often with high-pressure sales methods. To protect yourself against such problems, the experts advise you to take these steps:

- Call your local hospital and ask them to give you the telephone number of a local PERS dealer.

- Check the reliability of the dealer with your local Better Business Bureau. Ask if any complaints about product or service have been filed against the dealer.

- Find out whether it would be wiser to buy or rent (on a short-term basis, rental may be wiser). If you decide to rent, find out if you can cancel at any time if you are not satisfied.

What's Ahead in Senior Health Care?

The early 1990s were optimistic breakthrough years for retirees who like to look and plan ahead. Poet Robert Browning had given us an upbeat view of the future of older people with his immortal "Grow old along with me! The best is yet to be; the last of life for which the first was made." Still, many of us, especially in our early retirement years, were reluctant to accept the bittersweet fact that life itself is terminal.

The early 1990s brought needed reforms, long-awaited innovations (many described as 'miraculous"), and an impressive choice of alternatives to the old ways of living out our final years.

Nursing Homes

Although the U.S. now has more than 20,000 nursing homes, only about 5 percent of our older Americans live there. Nursing homes are closely regulated for the purpose of caring for people who are convalescing after a hospital stay, or who have chronic illnesses that require medical attention but not hospitalization, or who are too frail to live safely on their own.

About one-half of those admitted to nursing homes will stay less than six months. Only about 10 percent will stay three years or longer.

In 1990, after many studies of the quality of care in nursing homes, Congress passed legislation that brought sweeping changes in nursing home quality of life and quality of care, and required each state's Area Agency on Aging to have an Office of the Long-Term Care Ombudsman to handle complaints.

Choosing a Nursing Home

To find the right nursing home, the experts advise us to start with three basic questions: What kind of care is needed? What kind of lifestyle is preferred? And what is the best location for nearness to family, friends, and favorite visiting places?

149

Care divides into 24-hour-a-day *skilled* care and, for more mobile patients, *intermediate* care. Lifestyle means religious, ethnic, and other orientations.

It's suggested that we start by asking for referrals from a physician, social worker at the hospital, from a church or synagogue, or from the nearest Area Agency on Aging (see "Resources," Chapter 4). Telephone those homes and ask about rates, payment plans, activities, special facilities, policies about visiting, and other personal matters.

After narrowing our list to the most likely places, we are advised to make at least two personal visits to each home, including one at a different time of day and without any advance notice. It's a good idea, during those visits, to eat at least one meal, and to visit with the staff and the residents. We should judge the staff on professionalism and pleasantness, and judge the residents on their cleanliness and grooming, their cheerfulness — and their alertness. Apathetic residents can indicate a lack of recreational activities or overmedication.

Payment Plans

Nursing home costs are usually financed in one of four ways: 1) *Personal resources* (about one-half of all nursing home residents start this way, but often need other help soon). 2) *Private insurance*, either Medicare supplementary (Medigap) or long-term care insurance. 3) *Medicaid* (available in Medicaid certified nursing homes) for low-income individuals who need care at least above the level of room and board. 4) *Medicare hospital insurance (Part A),* available under some limited circumstances for a fixed period of skilled nursing home care, in nursing homes that are Medicare-certified.

Many health maintenance organizations (HMOs) and other coordinated care plans participate in the Medicare and Medicaid programs. In recent years, Medicaid has been covering about 60 percent of all nursing home costs. For people who are eligible, Medicaid also covers home health care services, medical supplies, and equipment.

For additional information on nursing homes, including check lists of what to look for, how to make complaints, and how to compare long-term insurance policies, write:

U.S. Department of Health and Human Services
Health Care Financing Administration
6325 Security Boulevard, Baltimore, MD 21207

American Association of Retired Persons
Health Advocacy Services
601 E Street, N.W.
Washington, DC 20049

Alternatives to Nursing Homes

To hold the line on senior health care costs, both for consumers and taxpayers, all federal and state governments are encouraging greater use of these lower-cost alternatives to nursing homes:

- Home Health Care
- Adult Day Care Centers
- Adult Foster Care
- Adult Congregate Living Facilities (ACLFs)
- Hospice Care

Home Health Care

Home equipment for the impaired person — from wheelchairs to adjustable beds to bath and toilet aids — can now be purchased or rented from specialty stores and giant chains. One special home health care catalog from Sears ran to 80 pages.

Hospital services — from tube feedings to blood transfusions to speech and physical therapy — have also moved into the home, along with the visiting nurse services that have been available for many years.

The familiar Meals-on-Wheels program delivers nutritious meals to homebound seniors. And Personal Emergency Response Systems (PERS) are available to assure the impaired person that help is always close at hand.

One of the most important of all breakthroughs in home health care is the increasing use of *blister packaging* for pills. Studies had indicated that an alarming percentage of people in nursing homes were there only because they could not be trusted to take the right pills at the right time. Blister packs, marked with times and numbers, now put pills of different colors on clear and easy-to-follow display. One drug company will even telephone the pill taker daily, at no charge, to be sure the pills are being taken properly.

The now-familiar *patches* are another innovative way of making sure the seniors are getting the right medication.

Adult Day Care Centers

Seniors whose families go out to work or who need a bit of respite from their home care duties can spend comfortable, safe days at the adult day care centers maintained by most Senior Centers and by many churches. The adult day care centers usually offer a variety of easy activities and are carefully supervised.

Adult Foster Care

Often referred to simply as "boarding homes," adult foster homes are private residences that take in seniors, usually just two or three, for their room and board. Adult foster homes must have a state license to receive Medicaid funding. They also accept private-pay boarders.

ACLFs

Adult Congregate Living Facilities (ACLFS) were described earlier in this book, in Chapter 9. They offer a wide variety of accommodations. Please turn back to Chapter 9 for a refresher.

Hospice Care

England's Dame Cicely Saunders, in 1967, introduced a new concept in health care at St. Christopher's in London. It was designed for patients with life-limiting illnesses and tried only to keep them comfortable, always free from pain, in homelike surroundings. The concept attracted worldwide attention and, in 1974, was adopted in the United States.

Hospice now offers not only physical comfort and freedom from pain — in the patient's home — but full-circle help with all the emotional, psychological, and spiritual concerns of both the patient and the family.

Hospice is a private, not-for-profit community service organization that specializes in caring for persons who have a life expectancy of one year or less, who are under the care of a physician who endorses the Hospice concept, and who have an on-site caregiver.

How Hospice Works

Hospice care is based entirely on need, not on ability to pay. There are no charges to the patient or family. Hospice funding comes from community giving, Medicare/Medicaid reimbursements, and from some private insurances. Hospice offers its service to the residents of the county in which the Hospice facility is operating, without regard for age, sex, religion, illness, handicap, or financial resources.

When a physician refers one of his patients to Hospice for in-home care, a personalized plan is drawn up to meet the patient's and the family's individual needs. The care plan may call for bi-weekly or monthly visits by Hospice nurses, home health aides, social workers, chaplains, and trained Volunteers.

The visits are concerned only with the patient's comfort, including freedom from pain. But the volunteer may elect to help with the family's shopping, may offer to keep the patient company while other family members go out for dinner or a movie, or may offer to take the patient out for a drive. The patient is always in charge.

For more information about Hospice, write to:

Hospice
1901 N. Moore Street
Suite 901
Arlington, VA 22209

Or call: 1-800-658-8898 (toll free).

Additional Comments

When our health care professionals look ahead to the year 2000, they agree on at least three basic points:

- The price of sophisticated, high-technology equipment will continue to exert strong upward pressure on health care costs.

- The longer life expectancy of our retirees will continue to heighten the load on all our health care facilities.

- If we are to cope successfully with the coming costs and demands, we must continue to emphasize preventive medicine, with its screenings and wellness programs, and we must rely increasingly on the self-help support groups and the expanding resources for home health care.

■ RETIRE SMART

Part V

What Would You Like to Do Today?

35

Make It a Four-Square Day

The choices, on Day One of retirement, can be bewildering. Where do we start? Sports, hobbies, arts and crafts, clubs, education, travel, a social whirl, and volunteer invitations all around.

Our veteran retiree friends all agree you need to do a lot of prioritizing or you'll lose a day, and then another, and then another. And you have no days or weeks to waste. We are always being reminded that yesterday is gone forever, and tomorrow may never come; so today is the only one we can count on for sure.

In this age of conscientious preretirement planning, it's probable that you have a firm schedule in hand for all your leisure-time activities. But if you're open to suggestions, here are four value measurements you may like to apply to each new day:

1. Make It Selective

Being selective is the first guideline for making the most of our time — and it applies to our thinking as well as our actions. We can live in the present or we can live in the past; but we can't do both at the same time. We can act or we can react; but we can't do both at the same time. We can be happy, or we can be sad; but we can't do both at the same time. We can love or we can hate; but we can't do both at the same time. We need to be selective because today is all we have.

2. Make It Useful

"Aging is a state of mind as well as body," says the National Institute of Mental Health. "Along with learning about new freedoms, you will be learning new roles. You have a great opportunity to choose activities that are self-fulfilling and at the same time worthwhile to the community."

3. Practice Discovery

Shelley Hegley, an authority on early-childhood education, stresses discovery along with self-esteem, self-discipline, and the other basic shapers of a new life. "Discovery," she says, "makes learning a joy — an uplifter. Discovery, as we grow older, becomes a continuous renewer." Once discovery becomes a habit, it supports a more interesting way of life. The conscious practice of discovery applies to everything we do, from planning a day's activities to scouting a new restaurant to dreaming up some new ideas for our next trip.

4. And Live Your Own Life

Dennis Oldham, an authority on gerontology, worries about a retiree problem that is becoming known as "lost selfhood." "For the first time in their lives," he points out, "couples are together nearly twenty-four hours a day. It can be a stifling kind of togetherness. One or the other can become so controlling that the mate begins to lose his or her sense of purpose. It can almost become a co-dependency problem needing professional help.

"Couples in retirement," Dennis Oldham says, "should consider planning activities apart from each other and live their own individual lives." He agrees with Shelley Hegley's point about discovery and adds: "Retirees need to learn to do things just for the sake of the enjoyment of doing them."

36

Your World of Reading

*T*he No.1 favorite of all retiree leisure time activities, according to a national survey among retirees by AARP, is *reading of all kinds.*

We took this up with the American Library Association, asking if they had any suggestions for making this pastime even more enjoyable and more fulfilling. They did.

Some Professional Tips

The head of the Association's Reference and Adult Services Division, Andrew M. Hansen, says one of a retiree's first acts should be to write down the *telephone number* of the local library's *reference department.* Next, he suggests that retirees visit the library to make a personal inspection of the various kinds of reference works that are available, including their formats. "The size of type," he points out, can be very important to readers whose eyesight may not be as keen as it once was — and one-volume encyclopedias and unabridged dictionaries may be too heavy for people with arthritic hands unless the books are on stands."

Mr. Hansen also recommends that you find out how extensively your library meets the range of your reading interests.

Your Library/Your Club

In many retirement communities, the local library has become a sort of private club with almost unlimited attractions: more varied magazines than we could ever afford to buy; historical works not available elsewhere; videos we can check out like books; and long shelves of books with titles that are stimulating to look at, whether or not we want to take one home.

The library is also a place for saving money: the how-to books and manuals can show us how to make many of our own repairs on cars, appliances, and other equipment.

And the cookbooks at a library can challenge anyone who eats, woman or man, to photocopy some new "discovery" recipes.

If your local library doesn't have some of the books you need, the librarian can suggest other sources, and may even offer to arrange for them to be sent from a library in another city in your state. Your librarian at the public library may also have occasion to remind you that you are welcome to visit the *law* library at the county courthouse if you need information on legal affairs.

The "What's New?" Place

To anyone who reads, today's book stores are spectacular, continuously-new "knowledge fairs" — and book stores are for browsing. Unless a reader makes a habit of visiting his favorite book store at least once a week, he can't be sure he won't miss a new title he has been hoping to see for himself or for a gift. It costs nothing to look over the new displays, lift some covers, and scan the *contents* pages. Book stores are where browsing began, and browsing can lead to some rare, life-enriching discoveries.

If you don't see a title you had hoped to see, ask the salesperson at the counter to run a quick computer check. Within a few seconds, your questions will be answered.

Timeless Reading

Some of our friends are like Leo Carlson of San Diego. As a career soldier, he never had time — he never stopped in one place long enough — to catch up on the reading he had always wanted to do. He went from World War II to the civil war in the mountains of Greece, then to the Middle East, then Vietnam . When he finally was able to assure Joan that the wars were all behind him, he made some inquiries and heard about the Great Books Reading and Discussion Program.

The Great Books Program grew out of the "Great Books Movement" initiated at the University of Chicago, in the early 1940s, by then-President Robert Hutchins. The movement was carried on by The Great Books Foundation, a non-profit educational organization based in Chicago. Some 2,000 Great Books clubs are now meeting regularly around the country, using reader aids and leaders' guides published and sold by The Great Books Foundation. The collection includes fiction and nonfiction. Some of the works are complete; others are portions of larger works. If it is inconvenient for a reader to join one of the clubs, he can buy copies of the books for at-home reading.

The "Great Books"

Here is a complete listing of the classic works that are covered in the Great Books Reading and Discussion Program:

THE GREAT BOOKS FOUNDATION
Programs of Interpretive Reading and Discussion for Adults

Introduction to Great Books
These collections of short fiction and nonfiction works can serve as an ideal introduction to the Great Books Reading and Discussion series.

First Series

WHY WAR? *Sigmund Freud*
THE MELIAN DIALOGUE *Thucydides*
THE SOCIAL ME *William James*
ROTHSCHILD'S FIDDLE *Anton Chekhov*
CONCERNING THE DIVISION OF LABOR *Adam Smith*
CHELKASH *Maxim Gorky*
HOW AN ARISTOCRACY MAY BE CREATED BY INDUSTRY *Alexis de Tocqueville*
OBSERVATION AND EXPERIMENT *Claude Bernard*
EVERYTHING THAT RISES MUST CONVERGE *Flannery O'Connor*
AN ESSAY IN AESTHETICS *Roger Fry*
AN OUTPOST OF PROGRESS *Joseph Conrad*
ON STUDYING *José Ortega y Gasset*

Second Series

POLITICS *Aristotle*
OF COMMONWEALTH *Thomas Hobbes*
BARN BURNING *William Faulkner*
OF CIVIL GOVERNMENT *John Locke*
IN EXILE *Anton Chekhov*
THE DECLARATION OF INDEPENDENCE
EQUALITY *Isaiah Berlin*
SORROW-ACRE *Isak Dinesen*
WHY AMERICANS ARE OFTEN SO RESTLESS *Alexis de Tocqueville*
AFTER THE BALL *Leo Tolstoy*
HABIT *William James*
THE OVERCOAT *Nikolai Gogol*

Third Series

ON HAPPINESS *Aristotle*
HABITS AND WILL *John Dewey*
HAPPINESS *Mary Lavin*
CRITO *Plato*
ON LIBERTY *John Stuart Mill*
CONSCIENCE *Immanuel Kant*
A HUNGER ARTIST *Franz Kafka*
OF THE LIMITS OF GOVERNMENT *John Locke*
ANTIGONE *Sophocles*
WHY GREAT REVOLUTIONS WILL BECOME RARE *Alexis de Tocqueville*
A ROOM OF ONE'S OWN *Virginia Woolf*
IN DREAMS BEGIN RESPONSIBILITIES *Delmore Schwartz*

Fiction selections are presented in their entirety; most nonfiction selections are taken from longer works.

The Great Books Reading and Discussion Program

First Series

CHEKHOV: *Rothschild's Fiddle* *
ARISTOTLE: *On Happiness*
PLATO: *The Apology* *
CONRAD: *Heart of Darkness* *
KANT: *Conscience*
MARX: *Alienated Labour*
BIBLE: *Genesis*
FREUD: *Civilization and Its Discontents*
ROUSSEAU: *The Social Contract*
DARWIN: *The Moral Sense of Man and the Lower Animals*
SHAKESPEARE: *Othello* *
HUME: *Of Justice and Injustice*
TOCQUEVILLE: *The Power of the Majority*
SIMMEL: *Individual Freedom*
SOPHOCLES: *Antigone* *

Second Series

PLATO: *The Crito* *
DEWEY: *The Virtues*
EURIPIDES: *Iphigenia at Aulis* *
ARISTOTLE: *Politics*
DOSTOEVSKY: *Notes from the Underground* *
BIBLE: *Exodus*
HOBBES: *Origin of Government*
MELVILLE: *Billy Budd, Sailor* *
SMITH: *Wealth of Nations*
SHAKESPEARE: *Antony and Cleopatra* *
KIERKEGAARD: *The Knight of Faith*
HERODOTUS: *The Persian Wars*
LOCKE: *Of Civil Government*
SWIFT: *Gulliver's Travels*
THOREAU: *Civil Disobedience* *

Third Series

DEWEY: *Habits and Will*
MILL: *On Liberty*
SHAKESPEARE: *Hamlet* *
BIBLE: *The Gospel of Mark*
THUCYDIDES: *History of the Peloponnesian War*
CLAUSEWITZ: *What Is War?*
CHEKHOV: *Uncle Vanya* *
MAIMONIDES: *On Evil*
HOMER: *The Iliad*
MONTESQUIEU: *Principles of Government*
CHAUCER: *The Canterbury Tales*
AESCHYLUS: *Agamemnon* *
JAMES: *The Beast in the Jungle* *
MACHIAVELLI: *The Prince*
TOLSTOY: *The Death of Ivan Ilych* *

Fourth Series

SCHOPENHAUER: *The Indestructibility of Our Inner Nature*
EURIPIDES: *Medea* *
WEBER: *The Spirit of Capitalism*
MOLIÈRE: *The Misanthrope* *
GIBBON: *The Decline and Fall of the Roman Empire*
BIBLE: *Job*
MILL: *Utilitarianism*
SHAW: *Caesar and Cleopatra* *
ST. AUGUSTINE: *The City of God*
PLATO: *Symposium*
MONTAIGNE: *Of Experience* *
DIDEROT: *Rameau's Nephew*
SHAKESPEARE: *The Tempest* *
HAMILTON, JAY, MADISON: *The Federalist*
GOGOL: *The Overcoat* *

Fifth Series

BIBLE: *Ecclesiastes*
SOPHOCLES: *Oedipus the King* *
FREUD: *On Dreams*
KAFKA: *The Metamorphosis* *
GOETHE: *Faust, Part One* *
KANT: *First Principles of Morals*
FLAUBERT: *A Simple Heart* *
HUME: *Of Personal Identity*
NIETZSCHE: *Thus Spoke Zarathustra*
DANTE: *The Inferno*
BURKE: *Reflections on the Revolution in France*
ADAMS: *The Education of Henry Adams*
SHAKESPEARE: *King Lear* *
ARISTOTLE: *On Tragedy*
PLATO: *The Republic*

Indicates complete work. All other selections are portions of larger works.

Some Introduction to Great Books selections are duplications of readings in the Great Books Reading and Discussion series.

For more information about the Great Books, write to:
The Great Books Foundation
35 East Wacker Drive
Suite 2300
Chicago, IL 60601-2298

Your Home Library

For your handy, continuing reference, our professional advisors suggest you keep these basic reference works on your shelves at home:

- **Dictionary.** If your present one is worn and overdue for replacement, visit your book store and see some of the fascinating new choices in the dictionary section. New words keep appearing in our changing language, you know, and a new dictionary can keep you smartly up with the times.

- **Atlas.** The world keeps changing. Your old atlas may not show the countries that are in the news today.

- **Almanac.** The first edition of *The World Almanac*, the best known of the general information almanacs, was published by the *New York World* in 1868. Recent editions contain nearly 1,000 pages of statistical and general information on almost every subject of national interest. *The World Almanac* currently ranks as America's No.1 best-selling book.

- **Encyclopedia.** An encyclopedia is defined as "a work that contains information on all branches of knowledge, usually in articles arranged alphabetically by subject." In addition to general encyclopedias, there are special encyclopedias on gardening, shop work, and other selective subjects. General encyclopedias are usually published in multi-volume sets, but some are available in single space-saver volumes.

- **Selected catalogs** and other handy reference works on subjects of special interest to you. We, for example, always kept a recent copy of the Sears, Roebuck catalog to show us quickly what classifications of products were currently available in the market place. We were saddened when the great old American "wishing book," an institution since 1886, was phased out in 1993.

- **The Yellow Pages.** Whether you keep it on a shelf or by your phone, the local Yellow Pages section of the telephone book is an essential timesaver. The Yellow Pages concept, an historic marketing idea, was first applied, in 1910, in Dayton, Ohio. It was the invention of Loren M. Berry, who had sold his mother's homemade horseradish from door to door as a boy and decided he would like to be a salesman.

- **Those 1-800 numbers.** More than 300,000 American businesses are now inviting toll-free calls over the 800 lines. The toll-free 800 concept, first tested by AT&T (American Telephone & Telegraph) in 1961, became a major, national communications service in 1965. Today, to find out if the company you want to contact has a toll-free 800 number, just pick up your phone and dial **800 information**: 1-800-555-1212.

37

Sorting Out Sports

*I*nformation about sports, in a retiree publication, always begins with a caution: see your doctor for a checkup before you begin any physical conditioning program. Dr. Louis J. Radnothy, who provided our risk factors chart in Chapter 17, always advises his retiree patients: "After fifty, be sure to keep one foot on the ground."

And our all-sports coach, Walter Colburn, from Jamestown, New York, always stresses the importance of preexercise stretching and warming up to avoid pulling or tearing a cold muscle.

Here is an at-a-glance guide to the vast array of sports and related physical activities available to you in retirement. Please note such inclusions as clogging and square dancing; they are here to remind you to discover some wholesome new exercises to add to your old favorites.

Sport	Benefits/Cautions	Added Remarks
Archery	Good for hand-eye coordination	Observe safety rules
Aviation — power	Great relaxer	Ask doctor about vision, hearing
Aviation — glider	Not recommended	Every landing can be a "crash landing"
Badminton	Good all-around exercise, but can be strenuous	Know when to slow down
Baseball	Not recommended	Too much risk of injury
Basketball	Good, but can be strenuous	Know when to slow down
Bicycling	One of the best	Always wear helmet
Billiards/pool	Good for hand-eye coordination	Also good for socializing
Boating — power	Gets you outdoors	Take safety course
Boating — sail	Gets you outdoors	Racing can be strenuous

Sport	Benefits/Cautions	Added Remarks
Boating — ice	Not recommended for beginners	Wear a helmet
Bowling	Good exercise and socializing	Caution: can aggravate old back, or knee problems
Clogging	Good rhythmic exercise	Good socializing
Croquet	Good flexing	Good socializing
Dancing — all types	Fine exercise	Great socializing
Fishing	Relaxing, but negligible exercise	Watch out for sunburn
Golf	Especially good if you do some walking	Also great for socializing
Hiking	One of the best	Know first aid
Hockey	Not for beginners	Wear helmet, pads
Horseshoe pitching	Improves coordination	Good unwinder
Horseback riding	Not for beginners	Know your mount, wear helmet
Jogging/running	Can be strenuous	Know when to slow down
Lawn bowling	Mild, outdoors	Good socializing
Ping-pong	Great for hand-eye coordination	Good socializing
Rowing	One of the best	Slow when tired
Scuba/snorkeling	Risky if you have had heart or emphysema problems	Also need professional training
Shuffleboard	One of the very best of easy, outdoor sports	Also one of the best for socializing
Skating roller/ice	Not for beginners	Wear helmet
Skiing — snow	Cross-country great; downhill too risky	Wear good sunglasses
Skiing — water	Can be risky	Follow all safety rules
Surfing	Can be dangerous	Wear jacket, watch for runouts
Swimming	One of the very best for the whole body	Also encourages involvement in aquacize
Tennis	Know your limitations	Slow when tired
Triathlons	Top test of physical fitness	Know your capacity, and when to slow down
Walking	One of the very best	See Chapter 24
Weightlifting	Static exercise, needs good warm-up	Stick with light weights

Learning More

Here are some excellent sources of additional sports information

Presidential Sports Award (all sports)
P.O. Box 68207
Indianapolis, IN 46268-0207

Senior Olympics (all sports)
U.S. National Senior Sports Organization
14323 South Outer Forty Road, Suite N300
Chesterfield, MO 63017

American Canoe Association
7432 Alban Station Blvd., Suite B226
Springfield, VA 22150

U.S. Cycling Federation
1750 E. Boulder St.
Colorado Springs, CO 80909

U.S. Fencing Association
1750 E. Boulder St.
Colorado Springs, CO 80909

U.S. Golf Association
Liberty Corner Road
Far Hills, NJ 07931

Ice Skating Institute of America
355 W. Dundee Road
Buffalo Grove, IL 60089-3500

U.S. Paddle Tennis Association
P.O. Box 30
Culver City, CA 90232

American Amateur Racquetball Association
815 N. Weber St.
Colorado Springs, CO 80903-2947

U.S. Rowing
201 S. Capitol Ave., Suite 400
Indianapolis, IN 46225

U.S. Ski Association
P.O. Box 100
Park City, UT 84060

U.S. Masters Swimming, Inc.
2 Peter Ave.
Rutland, MA 01543
(Send business-size SASE)

U.S. Volleyball Association
3595 E. Fountain Blvd., Suite 1-2
Colorado Springs, CO 80910-1740

American Water Ski Association
799 Overlook Dr. SE
Winter Haven, FL 33884

U.S. Weightlifting Federation
1750 E. Boulder St., Suite 205
Colorado Springs, CO 80909

38

The Rewards of Lifelong Learning

Jim Tilly, Mary McLeod, and Ron Paladini are just three of our many friends who have tapped the resources of the VoTech Centers and Community Colleges, with dramatic benefits.

Jim Tilly began his adult life as a combat paratrooper in World War II, retired as a master machinist in Troy, New York, and then dreamed of a second career as a writer.

Mary McLeod retired as a key executive in a Detroit advertising agency and looked forward to world travel.

Ron Paladini retired as a restaurateur in Patterson, New Jersey, still promising himself that he would somehow achieve something he had always wanted: a college education, complete with a degree.

In retirement, everything they wanted turned out to be within surprisingly easy reach.

Every retiree, for a variety of reasons, should be familiar with today's opportunities for lifelong learning. Two of those reasons are of *double* importance:

- Lifelong learning not only enhances the retiree's quality of life but his coping skills as well.

- Along with helping himself, the retiree will acquire some practical career guidance he can pass along to his children and grandchildren.

Vo-Tech Centers
Ever since the 1860s, the federal government has been working for a more democratic educational system in America. The pioneer land-grant colleges of agriculture and mechanics were followed in the 1900s by a national network of vocational-technical schools whose mission was to bring instruction in agriculture, homemaking, and the trades to the local level throughout America.

166

In 1963, the mission of the vo-tech centers was redefined to give them three major roles: 1) teaching basic occupational skills to newcomers to the workforce and to workers in need of retraining; 2) upgrading the skills of presently-employed workers to help them advance in their occupations; and 3) providing lifelong learning opportunities for all adults "in order to improve their competencies or enhance their quality of life."

The lifelong learning courses are so attractive to retirees that retirees now account for as much as 10% of the total enrollment at many vo-tech centers. In those vo-tech centers, the lifelong learning courses all have practical applications.

The Practical Approach

As fair-minded protection for all the younger people who are seeking jobs, or holding full-time jobs, the lifelong learning courses avoid what the vo-tech centers call "wage-earning skills." At the same time, the courses enable retirees to save money by learning more do-it-yourself skills, Here are some typical examples:

Engines for men. There's always good attendance, the vo-tech centers say, in courses that teach men how to maintain their outboards and their lawn mower engines. Auto mechanics and electronics courses are equally popular. Jim Tilly, machinist, headed for the courses in word processing and computers as aids toward a writing career.

Upholstery for women. "The courses in upholstery," the vo-tech people explain, "include making your own slipcovers. And you'd be surprised by the numbers of senior women who will be buying computers, to keep all their records, and want to learn more about computer operation." Still another high-demand course is the one for home health aides. That one draws many men as well as women.

Vo-Tech courses come in a variety of day and evening classes, and a variety of lengths, all at modest cost. Some are "open-entry" courses; you can start at any time while the course is in session. Retirees are invited to ask for free course catalogs at their nearest Vocational-Technical Center.

Community Colleges

According to James L. Wattenbarger, Distinguished Service Professor Emeritus at the University of Florida and a top national authority on the community college movement, today's community college was born as a "junior" college, in 1892, at the University of Chicago. It was the idea

167

of a young scholar named William Rainey Harper, who had founded the school with a gift of $2 million from his friend John D. Rockefeller and thus had a free hand to run things as he pleased.

President Harper divided his university into "senior" and "junior" colleges. The junior college was to be a transitional school between high school and the professional senior courses in the university. He then developed a nationwide plan for affiliated junior colleges. The first affiliate, the Joliet (Illinois) Junior College, opened in 1901.

Nationally, about 9 percent of all our people are within commuting distance of a community college. In Professor Wattenbarger's Florida, 99 percent of all residents are within commuting distance of a community college.

"In an interesting relationship," Professor Wattenbarger tells us, "populists *and* elitists in higher education were responsible for the growth of junior and community colleges. Populists wanted to provide access to higher education for the masses, while elitists hoped to *purify* higher education by providing separate institutions for the teaching of lower division students. In the years ahead, we estimate that about one-half of all Americans will take a course at a community college."

The Choice of Courses

Today's community colleges have three missions: 1) preparing some students to transfer to a 4-year college or university; 2) preparing other students for employment at the end of two years, with an associate degree; and 3) offering a choice of extended studies to the entire community.

"In serving the retiree population," one community college told us, "we ask for their suggestions for courses. Any group of eleven or more can ask for a course and we will do our best to line up an instructor to teach that course. In many cases, we will hold the classes in the adult parks where many retirees live."

The college, a typical one, offers credit and non-credit courses, and all fees are set at the break-even mark. Courses are offered in these categories:

Arts and crafts:
- Drawing and sketching
- Painting/pastel, oil and acrylic, watercolor
- Stained glass
- Quilting/beginning and advanced

- Floral arranging
- Dance/ballroom, jazz, ballet

Hobbies:
- Bridge/beginning, intermediate, advanced
- Antique collecting
- Gourmet cooking

Languages:
- Foreign languages
- American sign language
- Braille
- Writing for publication

Music:
- Beginning organ
- Easy techniques for organ, keyboard, piano

Computer — Beginning, intermediate, advanced

Health and safety:
- Healthy aging (video and film series)
- Massage therapy
- Nutrition and cholesterol control
- People's Medical School
  (series of lectures by physicians and other medical professionals)

Sports:
- Beginning tennis
- Beginning golf
- Scuba diving

Occupational update:
- Home health aide course
- Real estate refresher course
- Security guard training

Financial/legal:
- Investing wisely
- Wills, trusts, and estates
- People's Law School (series of lectures by judges, attorneys, and law
  enforcement officers)

Our friend Mary McLeod signed up at her community college for a foreign language course, and later took a second one. Our friend Ron Paladini signed up for credit courses leading to an associate's degree on his way to a 4-year university.

In addition to the Vo-Tech Centers and the community colleges, retirees have at least two other options in education to keep in mind for themselves and their friends:

High Schools/Adult Courses

Most high schools are now concentrating on the primary functions of helping drop-outs pursue diplomas and delivering basic education to adults who were not able to go beyond the early grades. Most high schools also are teaching English to foreign adults.

Elderhostel

Since its founding in 1975, Elderhostel has become the most successful senior education/travel program in America, offering short courses at more than 1,500 colleges. For a catalog of courses, write: Elderhostel, 75 Federal St., Boston, MA 02110.

Now Meet the Graduates

Jim Tilly, retired machinist, with writing talent plus new word processor and computer skills, found a trade journal publisher who needed editorial help. The publisher has since retired. Jim Tilly is the new publisher.

Mary McLeod, retired advertising executive, developed conversational ability in two major foreign languages and makes good use of them in her extensive travels abroad.

Ron Paladini, retired restaurateur, got a rousing ovation when he finished his course work at a 4-year university and received his bachelor's degree in psychological counseling, with high honors. The audience seemed both surprised and impressed to see a man in a cap and gown who needed a seeing-eye dog to lead him up the stairs and across the stage.

In all that great audience, only his former teachers and classmates knew that Ron Paladini had been totally blind since the age of 18.

39

Time for Travel

*O*n Sunday, January 25, 1959, amid a flurry of news reports that drew a massive crowd to the airport, American Airlines inaugurated the first coast-to-coast jet service, New York-Los Angeles. It was a heady, historic occasion.

For American's marketing team, it was also a terrifying time because they faced these facts: the huge jets, carrying twice the passengers at twice the speed, had suddenly quadrupled the number of seats to be sold. To make the awesome problem even worse, three-fourths of all U.S. adults, according to the surveys, were afraid to fly.

As one possible, partial way to avert impending doom, one young marketing staffer suggested: "Maybe we should go beyond the business travelers and the vacationers and go after the *retiree* market. They have the *time* for travel, and the *money*, and all the right *reasons*."

"Like what?" asked a senior associate.

"Like seeing their grandchildren. Like going to reunions. Like seeing the famous places they've always just read about."

"No way," said the senior associate. "You'll never get that many of the older people to get over their fear of flying. But I suppose it's worth a try."

That was back in 1959 and the young staffer was wiser than he knew. By the early 1990s, tourism had become the largest industry in the world, and about 80 percent of all leisure travel was being booked by people over 50.

Patricia Berlin Mitchell, who headed interior design at a famous university in New York City, now enjoys art museums in Europe, with her Robert as an always-agreeable ally. Mary McLeod, our Detroit advertising friend, is applying her new knowledge of foreign languages. Virginia and I received one of the best breaks of all when the International Executive Service Corps phoned one day and asked: "Could you and your wife leave next month for Jakarta? We have some volunteer assignments we think both of you will like. When you finish in Jakarta, you can just continue on and make it a complete trip around the world."

Retirement, for most people, is their very first chance to get out and see places they've been wanting to see all their lives. The sudden freedom to do it all can sometimes be intimidating. But the going, especially by air, can be easy.

Travel Agents

Many retirees are still not aware that travel agents are here to help us at no charge. They get their commissions from the transportation and hotel industries; but they are not obligated to any one company, so they can deliver impartial service. They can, for example, get you a better buy than you might get from dealing direct with one particular airline because a travel agent can shop around for the best available deals in any month or any week.

Most travel agents pride themselves on their first-hand knowledge of the places, the carriers, and the hotels they recommend. Some, of course, are more knowledgeable than others; so we have always made a practice of talking with several agents, not just one, about any important trip we are planning. We book, finally, with the one who showed the best knowledge of all the aspects of the trip, and who offered the best suggestions about things to see and do along the way.

As an important extra step in choosing your travel agent, always look for the credentials of a professional. The mark of a professional is a sign showing that the agent is a member of the American Society of Travel Agents (ASTA), the Association of Retail Travel Agents (ARTA), American Association of Travel Agents (AATA), the American Automobile Association (AAA), the International Air Transport Association (IATA), or Cruise Line International Association (CLIA). As a final precaution, ask if the agent is registered with the Airline Reporting Corporation (ARC), which requires a substantial bond from the agents who report to it. (The reason for taking precautions like these is that the booming tourism industry has attracted a few amateurs here and there.)

Make use of the no-charge help of the professional travel agents. They can be especially helpful, of course, on ambitious trips abroad — but they can also be surprisingly helpful on motor trips within your own state.

Air Travel

If you have never taken any long flights, here are some pointers that might be helpful: As protection against circulation problems, avoid garters and thigh-length girdles, drink plenty of fluids (non-carbonated and non-alcoholic), and try to get up and walk the aisles every 30-45 minutes. If you need a special diet on the flight, inform the airline within 24 hours of your flight. And it's wise, if you have had any history of heart or lung disease, diabetes, or thromboses, to get your doctor's OK before you fly because your pressurized cabin, on a long flight, will be comparable to atmospheric pressure at 5,000-8,000 feet above sea level.

The cargo bay, of course, is not pressurized, so pack shampoos and other possible "leakers" in ziplocked plastic bags.

And always remember, when you're taking a long flight, to reserve some quiet time at the end to rest up from jet lag.

Foreign Travel

If you have never taken any trips abroad, we suggest you check first with your doctor to see if you will need any special shots for the trip, and to arrange for refills of your prescriptions to take with you. (Then keep those medications in their original containers, for customs identification purposes, to avoid being suspected of bringing illegal drugs into a foreign country.) Along with your prescription drugs, you will want to carry remedies for irregularity, diarrhea, and upset stomach. Also, carry copies of any eyeglass prescriptions.

Next, start monitoring the weather at your destination. Be sure you will be taking the right clothes for keeping warm (or cool), and always carry light rainwear.

And it's a good idea, before you head for your travel agent, to make a detailed list of everything you want to discuss: the amount of local (foreign) currency you will need to have in your pocket when you arrive in certain countries; the amounts of duty-free purchases you can bring back; the procedures for renting (and insuring) rental cars abroad; and how to handle medical emergencies.

Your travel agent will be able to guide you through all the routine steps: passport photos, passport (for which you will need a certified birth certificate as proof of citizenship), the visas you will need, and a briefing on the special customs of the places you will visit.

As a follow-up on the travel agent's counsel, it's a good idea to visit your library, and your book store, and read all you can about the country or countries you will visit. Reading will remind you of many additional sights you would like to see while you're there. And then be sure you'll be ready to record all those sights for many repeat showings in the days and months and years to come. Take a camera or camcorder, and lots of film (print and slide) and tapes — what you need may not be readily available over there, or it might be very expensive.

Cruises

Of all the ways of traveling, cruises must easily rank as the most relaxing. You put your clothes on hangers and in *drawers* — a pleasant change from the living-out-of-a-suitcase feeling you've had on other trips. There's usually a great choice of pleasant activities and pleasant companionship, on board and when you go ashore at the various ports, and you usually feel pampered all the way. The dining alone can often be worth booking a cruise.

You'll want, of course, to take the right clothes for some of the ports, and some sea-sickness pills (just in case). If your cruise takes you to foreign ports, follow the precautions we just mentioned under "Foreign Travel."

Trains and Buses

Some essentials: Limit your luggage load to what you could handle alone if necessary. To add some additional easy-carry capacity, women should take multi-compartment purses, and men should wear shirts with double pockets.

For continuing comfort while "living in a seat," dress in "layers" — light street clothes backed by light sweaters, light jackets, and light rainwear you can toss in a rack.

Motor Trips

Most of our friends recommend joining the American Automobile Association (AAA) for the excellent maps, travel guides (including motel ratings), up-to-date routings, and emergency road service. Triple-A also offers the latest luggage and accessories (like money belts), and a continuing series of tour packages at reduced rates.

Elderhostel

We mentioned this education/travel organization in Chapter 38 on life-long learning and should mention it again here. Elderhostel provides short-term residential learning programs for adults 60 and over. The sessions are held throughout the United States and in more than 40 other countries. For more information, write to Elderhostel, 75 Federal St., Boston, MA 02110.

Traveling Alone

Our Detroit world traveler, Mary McLeod, has some upbeat comments for single women who worry about traveling alone: "It has never been a problem.

"Usually," she explains, "I have at least one good friend who shares my interest in certain trips and would like to go along. I plan ahead, so there's no last-minute rush to find a roommate.

"I do not advocate 'taking your chances' on a compatible roommate. Unless I know I have a congenial companion, I just pay the 'single supplement' and enjoy my evening privacy. On any group tour, I can always count on lots of good companionship the rest of the time. I have always felt welcome and never left out."

And Don't Forget Discounts

During most of every year, the senior travelers are the ones who keep the tourism industry healthy, and the industry shows its appreciation with a continuing stream of attractive discounts with no strings attached. So don't be bashful about checking the discounts before you sign for the service. Just to be sure you don't miss out on the substantial savings, get the 800 numbers for your favorite motel chains and call in advance with all your questions, including the one about discounts.

40

Brightening Your Mood with Music

As a young lawyer on horseback, riding his lonely circuit, Abraham Lincoln carried an old, well-worn harmonica to ease the emptiness. Harry Truman, with all the aftermath of WW II on his shoulders, turned to his piano. For them, music was a sure escape from loneliness and pressure.

"Yes," the professionals tell us, "but music is not just an escape from loneliness and pressure — it's also a great way to brighten your mood in lots of ways, and you don't need to know how to read or play a note to enjoy all the benefits."

Understanding Music

What we call "music" probably began when some unknown primitive person struck something hollow with a club and heard a strange sound. He repeated his beating, then tried it a little faster, then a little slower. It sounded good to him. He was pleased and should have been, because he had just invented *rhythm* — the *beat*.

Some later person found that the human voice, beyond being useful for communication, could also make pleasant high and low sounds. It was he (or she) who discovered *melody*. In time, the different levels of sound were called "notes." Then two singers, one with a high voice, the other with a low voice, sang the same melody, but using two levels of notes that sounded good together, and *harmony* was born.

"That's all there is to music," the professionals explain, "the three basic components are *melody, harmony*, and *rhythm* — and you can appreciate it all intuitively, without ever being taught. Music is something you feel with an inner sense and respond to. You know when the sounds are pleasantly harmonious, and when they are just discordant noise.

"And all you have to do, to start enjoying all this, is to switch on your radio and do some experimenting with the tuner."

Radio Is Everywhere

Radio, long called "the companion medium," now operates in "formats," with one format per station per area. Typical formats: Adult Contemporary, Classical, Contemporary Hits, Country, Easy Listening, Jazz, Oldies, Religious, and Rock. Somewhere along that spectrum, there's some music your inner person would like to hear, because nothing can lift your spirits faster than music.

Radio is your musical shadow: in your living room, bedroom, kitchen, car, and even going along with you on your walk.

If you don't have a favorite station, treat yourself to a go-anywhere cassette player and pick up some extra cassettes for your car. Do some browsing through stores that sell records, tapes, and compact discs the way you browse through book stores.

Music is a magic carpet with no time or distance limitations. Would you like for a while, to be back in your school days? Your courting days? Your favorite Broadway show times? Would you like, for an hour or so, to be back in candlelit colonial times, hearing the sounds of the harpsichord and the chamber strings? Just listen. Music will take you there.

Can You Sing?

During the 1920s and 1930s, radio was taking over so much of the musical universe that one of America's earliest and original musical forms was in danger of fading away. The musical form was barbershop quartet singing. Born in rural America during the Saturday nights of the 1840s, barbershop harmonizing was soon picked up by the minstrel shows and went on to a glorious peak in vaudeville. Then came radio. People had so much music to listen to, they began to forget singing.

The impending demise of barbershop harmony was deeply troubling to one loyal barbershopper in Tulsa, Oklahoma, named Owen Clifton Cash. He shared his fears with fellow Tulsan Rupert I. Hall and they agreed something must be done. They admitted that the problem did not qualify as a national crisis, so it should be presented with a bit of tongue-in-cheek humor.

The year was 1938, replete with the New Deal's "alphabet soup" of such initialed federal agencies as CCC, WPA, and NRA, so Cash and Hall decided to top all the other initials with their own set: *SPEBSQSA*. An alert reporter from the *Tulsa Daily World* put it on the news wires. The response was immediate.

SPEBSQSA, which stands for "The Society for the Preservation and Encouragement of Barber Shop Quartet Singing in America," now has more than 35,000 members throughout the United States and Canada, and has affiliates in nine foreign countries, including one in the former Soviet Union.

Barbershop harmony is a style of unaccompanied singing with four voice parts: lead, tenor, baritone, and bass. The lead usually sings the melody. The tenor harmonizes above the melody. The bass sings the lowest harmonizing notes and the baritone provides in-between notes, either above or below the lead, to complete the chords that give barbershop its distinctive, four-part sound.

Inevitably, as the barbershop harmony society was on its way to becoming the world's largest all-male singing fraternity, there was a need for a companion organization for women. The "Sweet Adelines" now fill that need, and there is a third organization for barbershoppers in Canada. For further information, our readers are invited to write to:

- SPEBSQSA, Inc., 6315 Third Ave., Kenosha, WI 53143-5199

- Sweet Adelines International, P.O. Box 470168, Tulsa, OK 74147

- Harmony, Inc., 511 Cameron St., Dalhousie, New Brunswick EOK 1BO

Can You Play an Instrument?

Long before we became intimidated by such instruments as the violin, the tuba, and the multi-reed church organ, we learned that anybody who could hum could play a kazoo. Later, in childhood, we saw people become famous by tapping, xylophone style, on the bent side of a common saw. Much later, after WW II, we saw how the residents of some Caribbean Islands invented an ingenious new form of music by converting abandoned U.S. Navy oil barrels into steel drums. Music can be made in almost any way you want to make it.

Retirees who never played a note before are now discovering what the lonesome cowboys learned long ago — that we can make all sorts of companionable, memory-enriching music by just using three chord-making fingers, and some strumming fingers, on the six strings of a go-anywhere guitar. The country music that has captivated America seldom calls for more than three different chords.

Still other retirees are discovering the handbell choirs that have sprung up everywhere. In a handbell choir, you might have to play only a single note — or possibly two or three — but don't dismiss that as too simple. The teamwork of a handbell choir can be a spectacular performance to watch as well as hear.

Playing the BIG Instrument

The conductor of a world-famous symphony orchestra was once asked by a reporter if he, the conductor, played a musical instrument. "Yes," the conductor said haughtily, "I play the *big* instrument."

"You mean the entire orchestra?" asked the reporter.

"Yes," said the conductor, "I play the entire orchestra."

Today's good news is that every senior citizen, within easy weeks, can be playing "the *big* instrument" in the form of an electronic organ or its incredible little cousin, the portable keyboard.

We asked our favorite self-taught musician, Paul Heinsohn, to explain how easy it is. Paul, who learned all his music in Birmingham, Michigan, failed early and miserably at the piano. Later, when he wanted to join the high school band, the bandmaster decided Paul's musical talents extended only to beating the big drum. Still later, when he went on the road as a sales representative for one of the major automobile companies, often rolling up more than 5,000 miles a month, Paul suddenly felt a desperate need for some sort of *unwinder* whenever he reached home.

His wife, Barbara, suggested he try the Hammond Organ. He did — and was so impressed by the ease of learning to play it that he decided to make a career switch from cars to organs. Paul's predecessors, in the automobile business, had sold the cars by first teaching the prospective customer how to drive. Paul Heinsohn sold organs by teaching people how to play one.

We asked Paul if he would outline, for our readers, the introduction he used to give to his prospective customers. He said he would and here it is, by the numbers.

Introducing the Keyboard

1. Visit a musical instrument dealer who sells electronic keyboards and ask to see a beginner's "big note" music book for the keyboard. You won't need your reading glasses to see the giant notes and chord guides.

2. With one finger of your right hand, play one of the book's tunes that is familiar to you. Notice how an organ note compares with a piano note. A piano note "decays" (fades out); an organ note keeps playing until you are ready to move on to the next note. You're never rushed. (Later, you'll learn how that single finger can play five notes at one time.)

3. With one finger of your left hand, play a chord. A graphic chord guide, which you can place over the keys for a while, makes it easy to learn the chords. (Later, to play a tune like Silent Night, you'll be using only three different chords. To play a tune like Beautiful Dreamer, you'll use only four chords.)

4. Now select a sound and listen to the kind of accompaniment you can have with your two-finger playing. Choose from sounds like clarinet, strings, Hawaiian guitar. Makes you feel like the conductor of an orchestra, doesn't it?

5. Finally, be aware that the keyboard has an "auto play" feature — but don't use it yet. The auto play feature will provide your rhythm later — like having your own drummer. But hold the automatic beat for later — it sets the pace and, in the beginning days, you might not be able to keep up with it.

More about the Keyboard

Paul Heinsohn, the self-taught master of the organ, has these special compliments for the electronic keyboard:

• It is light, small, portable and easy to store
• It has its own speakers for amplification, or you can plug it into your home stereo system for real "auditorium sound"
• You can also listen to it with earphones in a silent room
• You can use the keyboard's memory to program what you play and then play it back, player piano style, as often as you like

Paul has just two cautions: 1) Be sure the keyboard you buy has standard-width keys; some keyboards have extra-narrow keys, which can lead to mistakes. 2) Have fun with your keyboard — alone and with your friends — "it was never meant to be taken seriously."

41

Let Mother Nature Guide Your Gardening

"The kiss of the sun for pardon,
The song of the birds for mirth;
One is nearer God's heart in a garden
Than anywhere else on earth."

Among all our green-thumb gardening friends, nobody knows who wrote the delightful verse above, but they all agree with everything it says. Most of them have it posted, as a metal sign, in the midst of their flowers.

Gardening, for our retiree friends, is a creative and peaceful pursuit with uplifting and healing powers for the mind, the body, and for our outlook on the world about us.

It can also be a great enhancer of our self-esteem because the private act of gardening is also a very public one. A friend who runs a garden shop once told us, "You can take pride in a lot of things in and around your home, but the most visible things about it, to everyone else, are your lawn and your plantings."

Our Miami friend Ann Marie Martin, for example, was a prominent person in retail advertising there; but she has won even greater renown, in retirement, for her colorful beds of gardenias, roses, azaleas, daylilies, and exotic orchids.

And our Cleveland friend Vincent Mahany, even before he retired from the paint industry, had won a number of the highest honors his fellow Masons could bestow on him. But he and Mildred made some of their best-remembered impressions on their Masonic friends throughout Ohio with their gift baskets of plump, juicy tomatoes from the Mahany garden.

Timely Tips

Mother Nature has three suggestions for retirees:

1. The master gardeners of your County Extension Service are waiting to help you with free literature, free seminars, and continuing
   availability, over the phone, for all your questions. They also will
   be glad to put you on a mailing list to receive periodic bulletins,
   usually at no charge.

2. You are invited to join one of the numerous garden clubs in
   retirement areas — men's as well as women's.

3. If you are moving to a new locality, please check with the local
   master gardeners before you start planting all the things you used
   to plant "back home." Growing conditions can often change within
   relatively short distances. So go along with Mother Nature in your
   gardening. She knows what grows best where you live now. Do it
   her way, not your way. Her way is easier. And greener. And more
   rewarding.

Biking Rolls into an Exciting New Era

When England's H.J. Lawson invented the chain-driven bicycle in 1876, he claimed only that its wheels and sprockets ran in perfect alignment, and all bearings were parallel to one another and to the direction of travel. It apparently never occurred to the modest man that the basic design would remain unchanged for more than a century, and that he would be leaving a priceless engineering legacy to humankind.

Ironically, it's only now that the bicycle is coming in for its highest acclaim...especially among retirees.

- In the midst of world concern about energy conservation, the experts have determined that, in terms of energy consumed per mile, the efficiency of the chain-driven bicycle is comparable to that of an automobile delivering 1,000 miles per gallon of gasoline — and with no pollution.

- Cardiovascular authorities are honoring the bicycle as "one of the very best ways of getting aerobic exercise to strengthen the heart and lungs."

- Orthopedic specialists are recommending bicycle exercise for people who shouldn't be subjecting their joints to high-impact aerobics.

To make today's biking even more attractive, the national Rails-to-Trails movement has now passed the 500-trails mark, reaching through more than 30 states, in its drive to preserve abandoned railroad rights of way and convert them into greenway trails for bikers, hikers, skiers, and equestrians.

So there's never been a better time than now to do some browsing in bicycle stores. The basic design of the Lawson chain-driven bicycle has continued unchanged for more than a century, but there's been a revolution of refinements in the lighter-but-stronger frames, gears and gear-shifting, brakes, handlebars, tires, and safety equipment.

Choosing the Right Model

You have a choice of bicycles and tricycles. The bicycles let you choose a one-speed (coaster brake) bike for flat-country riding, or a multi-speed bike, with up to 24 speeds, for easy pedaling on even the steepest hills. You can have upright handlebars for a better view of traffic, or "dropped" handlebars for greater speed. You can have the familiar rear coaster brake (applied by pushing backward on the pedal) or front and rear hand brakes. You also have a choice of toe clips and straps to keep your feet more secure on the pedals.

You can look enviously at the high-performance racing and triathalon models — and the highly popular mountain bikes — but you'll probably feel safer and more comfortable later with a touring model with balloon tires, not the lean racing tires. The "fat" tires not only deliver a softer ride but are safer and more stable whenever you have to veer off the road into grass or gravel.

Tricycles are heavier and slower, but steady and very comfortable, with a generous capacity for carrying groceries and packages. One of the more popular models is called the "side-by-side." It has two sets of pedals and chains for couples who would like to ride side-by-side and take turns pedaling.

Talk in advance with your biking friends, and talk with the cycle center people, about the best choice of cycle and accessories for the kind of riding you plan to do.

Safety Equipment

Helmet. The majority of serious cyclist injuries and deaths are head-related, so your most important safety purchase is a quality helmet with a hard outer shell, a crushable liner that absorbs shock, and a strong strap and buckle. Make sure your helmet carries an approval sticker from the Snell Memorial Foundation or ANSI (American National Standards Institute). It's easy to be spilled unexpectedly by a rut, pothole, oil smear, or roaming dog, and your head, even at slow speeds, can suffer permanent damage.

In addition to the protective cover, a helmet adds to your safety by making you more quickly visible to motorists, especially in bad light. You can add to the visibility with retro-reflective trim tape. Smart bikers also carry identification and emergency information on tape inside their helmets. A good helmet should be bright in color, a comfortable fit, and should not interfere with your vision or hearing.

Lights. In any riding you do after dark, your state probably requires a white front headlight and a red rear taillight (in addition to the rear reflector), either powered by a battery or by a generator turned by a tire.

Also desirable: A retro-reflective vest, rear-view mirror, reflective tape on pedals and other surfaces, a bright orange flag on a rod at the rear, a tire pump, a safety lock, and, of course, an ankle clip, if you wear long pants, to keep them from being snagged by the chain.

Comfort Equipment

For any biking beyond an easy swing around the park, you're sure to want a soft saddle cover, either sheepskin or gel, and padded inserts for your pants.

For trips of any distance, in addition to a water bottle, you will want a gear duffel bag and a filter bottle that will let you drink safely from streams and ponds.

Safety Rules

Your state probably defines your bicycle as a vehicle. As its driver, you must obey all the rules that apply to other drivers. Before you ride anywhere, ask your cycle dealer, motor vehicle office, or police department for a copy of the state laws, local ordinances, and schedule of fines for various violations (some are shockingly stiff). Always follow these rules:

Ride with traffic. All 50 states require cyclists to go with the traffic flow, never against it.

Stop at stop signs and stop lights.

Before you turn, always look back, check for traffic, then extend your left arm for a left turn, your right arm for a right turn.

Yield to pedestrians in a crosswalk, or when riding on or across sidewalks. Note: adult riders should stay off sidewalks.

No headsets. Do not wear a headset, headphone, or any other listening device except a hearing aid when riding.

Bells, horns. Don't expect motorists to hear them. Always be ready to yell a warning.

Maintenance. Read and follow the instructions in your owner's manual.

Learning More
Look for bicycling magazines at your newsstand or book store. Examples: *Bicycling, Bicycle Guide.* Also, most major cities have a bicycling club, where retirees are always welcome. Check locally for bicycle information at the American Automobile Association and at cycling centers.

Rails to Trails
Every year, across the United States, railroads are abandoning more than 3,000 miles of track. The Rails-to-Trails Conservancy, a non-profit, Washington-based advocacy group, is trying to persuade public officials at all levels to preserve all the abandoned rights of way for possible future mass transit use and, in the meantime, to use the rights of way for a national network of greenway trails for hiking, cycling, skiing, and horseback riding. A mere 200 acres of right of way can provide a park more than 20 miles long.

America, by 1920, had the largest railroad system in the world, with over 250,000 miles of track. Against competition from cars, trucks, buses, and airlines, many famous old rail corridors are now becoming littered wasteland or a part of urban sprawl.

What is now the national Rails-to-Trails movement began in the 1960s, in communities scattered throughout America, where concerned citizens worried about the future of green space and wildlife, and outdoor recreation for their children.

In 1985, trails enthusiasts created the Rails-to-Trails Conservancy as a non-profit organization and soon had the backing of environmentalists and conservationists, and such influential organizations as the American Association of Retired Persons and the American Lung Association, from coast to coast. Almost every state now has at least one rail-trail. Michigan now leads with nearly 50, followed by Pennsylvania, Wisconsin, Iowa, California, Washington, Illinois, New Hampshire, and Minnesota.

Congress Is Helping
In 1983, Congress created a "rail-banking" program, which designated abandoned rail corridors as future train routes, but permitted their in-

terim use as recreational trails. Many individuals have challenged the rail-banking program, but the Supreme Court ruled in 1990 that rail banking was a valid use of Congressional power. Congress helped again with its Intermodal Surface Transportation Efficiency Act of 1991, which earmarked $151 billion for creating and improving rail-trails.

Rail-trails have special appeal to retirees because the old railroad builders sought out no-grade or slight-grade "water-level" routes along the shores of rivers and lakes. Along with the easy exercise, these trails offer a bonus of beautiful scenery and a relaxing escape from traffic turmoil.

For more information about the Rails-to-Trails effort in your area, send your inquiry, along with a stamped, self-addressed envelope, to: Rails-to-Trails Conservancy, 1400 Sixteenth St., NW, Washington, DC 20036

43

Tracing Your Ancestry

When our Tampa friend Leon Clark retired from his personnel post at Florida's massive MacDill Air Force Base, he and Betty decided to spend a whole summer, if necessary, finding out where and how the Clark family had settled in America. He knew only that some of the Clarks had made it to the town of Lee, in Massachusetts. There the trail ended.

So Leon and Betty drove to Lee, where they found a helpful historical society that gave them a clue that led to a newspaper in Pittsfield, where they picked up another clue that led to the historical museum in Northampton, where they found the rest of the story. As their final stop, Leon and Betty visited the local cemetery where ancestor William Clarke (with an "e") was honored with an impressive monument. He had landed in America in 1630, had helped to found the town of Dorchester, and then had served as a selectman in Northampton, where he also built a grist mill. With all the help of history-minded Massachusetts, Leon and Betty were able to write a fine report.

"That was something I owed my family," Leon told us. "If somebody like me doesn't look it up, who will? I've always been curious about it — now I have the time to check it out."

Our friend Jeannette Jones Phethean chose a much more difficult project. From her home in West Pittston, Pennsylvania, she wanted to trace ancestors in Scotland and Wales — and had no family information to start with. By the time she finished (and successfully), she was qualified to teach genealogy classes and write a popular newspaper column on genealogy in her retirement city.

Where to Begin
After Jeannette Jones Phethean had checked out virtually all the recommended sources of information, she ranked her most helpful sources in

this general order of importance to her:

1. Relatives who may have family information — in their files, their Bibles, or their memories — or who can refer you to still another relative who may have the information.

2. The Family History Centers of the Church of Jesus Christ of the Latter Day Saints, known as the Mormon Church.

3. Genealogy magazines. "Answer the queries in those magazines; you can learn a lot about genealogy by helping others with their research."

4. Local libraries. "Ask about the interlibrary loan privilege on microfilm."

5. Cemetery records.

6. National Archives, Washington, DC 20408. "You might need to go to the National Archives in person to get the information you need."

"Next to reading," she adds, "letter-writing is most important. Every trip I make to the mailbox is full of anticipation, and every letter from a newly-found relative is an exciting event."

For more information about genealogical studies, ask your librarian and book store for their recommendations. Meanwhile, here are three of Jeannette Jones Phethean's favorites:

• Arlene Eakle: The Source

• Val Greenwood: Researcher's Guide to American Genealogy

• Harriet Stryker-Rodda: How to Climb Your Family Tree

44

The Quilting Bee Is Back

*F*or a few long minutes, after we step into the big room, it feels like a return to colonial times. This is the weekly meeting of the local Quilters Guild, with 36 women around big tables, moving patiently through the stages of transforming little patches of multicolored fabric into a luxurious quilt.

"This can look very confusing at first," says our guide. "It takes about fourteen hundred of those little patches to make a quilt. But when you finish, you have a one-of-a-kind keepsake nobody would ever want to part with."

The women range in age from the mid-30s into the 80s, and some are here for the first time. Each newcomer, we're told, is paired with an experienced quilter for easy learning.

Our guide says quilting has been experiencing a big revival ever since the bicentennial of 1976. "It's a unique kind of activity," she says. "It's a combination of craftwork, socializing, and the creating of something very distinctive. When you're quilting, it takes your mind off all the petty things. You're thinking ahead, all the while, about the person who will be receiving that quilt as a loving gift. And you're working, side by side, with other congenial people who feel the same way. When you're quilting, you're never lonely."

The Home Quilter

Sid Pittman, our friend in Granbury, Texas, writes that his wife, Connie, is now doing more *lap* quilting than *frame* quilting "because it takes a sewing room of about 14X14 feet to do frame quilting right. For lap quilting, you just use different size *hoops* to make your round or square *blocks*. Then you sew them all together to make the quilt.

"I'm helping her now on a Christmas quilt, and she has some friends who are interested in getting started. They may end up starting another Guild chapter."

Joining the Guild

Sylvia Pickell, President of the National Quilting Association, has this advice for beginners: "Buy several of the quilting magazines to find out what is going on in your area. Then visit a fabric or quilt shop and ask about instruction geared to your interests. After that, go to the quilt shows and participate in local classes and workshops.

"Our headquarters is in the Howard County Center for the Arts in Ellicott City, Maryland, and we invite your readers to visit us there. We have a reference library and an exhibit gallery with quilts on loan from almost everywhere. We now have more than 250 chapters and offer individual and group memberships. The members receive full-color newsletters."

For more information, send a stamped, self-addressed envelope to: The National Quilting Association, Inc., P.O. Box 393, Ellicott City, MD 21041-0393

45

Art for Your Sake

"**B**eauty," they say, "is in the eye of the beholder." And "art," according to the dictionary, is simply "the conscious use of skill, taste, and creative imagination in the production of aesthetic objects." Coming full circle, "aesthetics" is defined vaguely as "relating to the beautiful."

Does all this mean that art is a place where anything goes?

We put the question to our favorite professionals in the working world of art and their answer is: "Yes...*almost.*"

Patricia Berlin Mitchell, our interior designer friend in New Jersey, whose paintings have been exhibited here and abroad, says: "The whole idea is to enjoy the creative process. You do it for your own inner satisfaction. But I would offer a few cautions."

Lurabel Colburn, our art teacher friend from Jamestown, New York, who is also a distinguished portrait artist, says: "Your average retiree just wants something he can do fast and take home tonight, and that's fine with me. But I would offer a few cautions."

The Cautions

1. Much as you might dislike rules, take time to learn the basics about composition and perspective, just to avoid being disappointed with the results you get. Says Lurabel:

> "I always encourage my students to learn how to draw the basic shapes — spheres, cones, prisms, cubes — and then to learn light and shadow."

2. Avoid using a medium that might seem fast, but can give disappointing results. Patricia and Lurabel offered these specifics:

"Acrylics dry fast and you can carry them home that day — but they don't blend well because they dry darker than what you apply, so it's almost impossible to match colors later. Oils are more forgiving — it's easy to match colors later, even after several days.

"Watercolors appeal to a lot of beginners because they're cheap. But then comes the disappointment: watercolors are too final — once they're on, they're on to stay."

3. Avoid trying to do too much too fast — you risk being discouraged. "Start with still lifes, not with anatomy."

Where to Start

Patricia and Lurabel, and others we talked with, all agree that retirees would do well to visit their nearest community college and ask about the art classes being offered, and then to see what other classes are being offered by various independent artists on a group or individual basis. "It's great," they say, "to be in a congenial group of beginners and intermediates — with a patient instructor — because you can learn so much from one another. And it ought to be fun!"

Working with Wood

As part of preparing a son for the working world, every good father always taught him how to saw a straight cut across a board and smooth out rough spots with a plane.

Now, at retirement time, we are learning that working with wood can be magical medicine for the brain, the body, and the spirit.

The World of Wood Carving
Barry Miner taught wood carving at a prestigious New England school for gifted children with other handicaps. Now he teaches retirees. "The kids," he tells us, "were near-geniuses with calculators and computers, but they had no hand-eye coordination. Wood carving helped their coordination, and taught them many other good things."

And what was it doing for the seniors? "It may be hard to believe," says Barry, "but I have one student, still in his sixties, who had lost all his self-confidence. He just felt totally useless, not needed any more. When he first came to our wood carving club, he was stuttering — something he had never done before. That was three months ago. Now his self-confidence is back and the stuttering is gone."

Wood carving in America began with a few artists and many whittlers, here and there, who were just whiling away the time. Now the National Wood Carvers Association mails its bimonthly magazine to more than 40,000 members. In retirement areas, wood carving clubs with as many as 200 members are not uncommon, with about equal numbers of men and women. "The only difference between men and women members," we're told, is: "the men like bigger, bolder projects and the women are better at the finer details."

"Carving wood," said one typical member, "is an easy way to concentrate on what you're doing and forget all your worries. And it's easy to get into wood carving because you can start with a single knife and some throwaway wood, and you can do it on any kind of table or bench."

194

Tools and Woods

In wood carving, there is no official rule about tools, but there is general agreement that a good starting kit consists of a mallet and six small chisels: two sizes of straight chisels, one slant-blade skew chisel, one U-gouge chisel, and one V-gouge chisel. You'll soon be adding to your collection with a carver's bench knife, various saws, some rasp-like shaper tools, a buffing wheel to help you keep the tools sharp, and either a conventional or a "power-arm" vise to hold what you're carving. A power-arm vise is not really powered; it is simply a manually-tightened vise that is multi-directional and flexible — it can swivel around to hold your wood in a vertical, horizontal, or diagonal position. All carving tools are available at hardware and hobby stores.

Favorite woods among carvers are: white and sugar pine (not yellow pine; too hard), basswood, black walnut, butternut, cherry, chinaberry, magnolia, and mahogany. Carvers tend to think maple and oak are too hard. And when newcomers ask, "Isn't mahogany an imported wood? Isn't it pretty expensive for carving?" the carvers' response is: "We get scraps from the makers of doors and other mahogany products — the scraps they usually just burn or throw away."

Veteran carvers advise: "Keep in touch with your local tree surgeons and landscapers. You're looking for *chunks* of wood, not just boards. The best chunks for carving are often wood that's being thrown away."

Subjects for Carvings

"Start with something simple and *finish* it," say Barry Miner and the other carvers. "That's the way to build confidence in yourself. Don't try a human figure; you'll probably make one arm shorter than the other. Don't try a human face; you'll probably wind up with two eyes that don't match."

The favorite subjects among beginners — and even among the old pros — are folk figures: cowboys, fisherfolk, rustics, hoboes, urchins. They're basically cartoon characters, so you can carve as you please with no worries about accuracy.

In every case, you start with some rough cuts with saws to get a general shape, and then start chipping and carving.

Animals are another favorite subject. Start with the head of a dog, cat, horse, alligator (pick any favorite), or with an animal at rest. When you become a member of the National Wood Carvers Association and start exhibiting your work in one of the hundreds of shows they put on around the country, you can try a Remington-type cowboy on a bucking bronco, or an exotic bird in a lacy tangle of branches — but not yet. Don't start anything you can't finish.

When you start finishing some carvings you're proud of, you'll stain or paint them and send them out as gifts. Wood carvings are unique and highly personal. Gift carvings usually are given an honored place on a display shelf and are never thrown away.

For more information about wood carving and wood carving clubs, ask your local hobby stores or write: National Wood Carvers Association, P.O. Box 43218, Cincinnati, OH 45243.

D-I-Y Projects

We live in what sociologists call the Do-It-Yourself Age, D-I-Y for short. Be glad we do. Away back in 1854, philosopher Henry David Thoreau warned that "Americans, as they become industrialized, risk becoming the tools of their own tools."

One century after Thoreau's warning, we were in the age of "quick 'n' easy" foods ("just add water and bake"), to which conscientious homemakers soon rebelled, saying they were tired of being treated like idiots.

Along with the quick 'n' easy foods came throwaway products that could not be repaired, only discarded. Individuals with even the slightest spark of creativity ultimately felt as though they were being phased out by a roboticized society.

Inevitably, the stifling of creativity inspired a massive wave of do-it-yourselfing. And wood was born for the D-I-Ys.

Do-it-yourself woodworking ranges from household objects we make and use to keepsake gifts to money-saving remodeling and repairs.

D-I-Y Tools

You start with a workbench (which you can buy or make), then add whatever basic tools you need for a project that appeals to you. You need at least one type of saw, a rasp-like shaping tool and a plane, a manual or electric boring tool, a hammer, screwdrivers, and a tape rule or other measuring device. All the guidance you'll need is readily available at your local hardware store, home center, and mass merchandiser's tool department.

In a retirement community, where noise is often offensive to the close-by neighbors, you can use such hand tools as rabbet and router planes to do what you might have thought you needed power tools to make.

Popular Things to Make

One favorite first project is a versatile workbench that can be folded to a neat package only six inches thick for easy storage in closet or garage. Another is a handy "anything chest" that holds just about anything and doubles as a coffee table. Just leaf through the guidebooks and pick out something your home would like to have.

Outdoor projects are still another big challenge: chaise lounges and lawn chairs, patio tables and benches, and even a gazebo.

And there's no end, of course, to the playthings a do-it-yourselfer (man or woman) can make for the grandchildren. Handmade toys are often kept for a generation or even longer, and the giver is fondly remembered.

Mr. Fixit Work

For any retiree who would like to turn an old bargain home into a thoroughly modern one — or who would like to save money for a boat or car instead of using it to pay repair bills — a good kit of tools can be worth a small fortune. Any guidance you need is readily available, either in a book or at your nearest Vo-Tech Center. The only project a beginner is advised not to try is one involving electrical or plumbing work.

For more information about D-I-Y projects, check your newsstand and hobby shops for D-I-Y publications. Also, an excellent source is Stanley Tools. Stanley publishes a variety of guidebooks, including *You-Can-Do-It Projects*, a collection of nine projects. For a copy, mention the book title and send your check or money order for $2.00 (which will also cover postage and handling) to: Stanley Tools, Advertising Services Department, P.O. Box 1800, New Britain, CT 06050.

Playgrounds for Children

In 1990, some two dozen professionals from around America got together and formalized what is now called the *community-built movement*. It had been growing slowly for about two decades, as a revival of the pioneer customs of barn raising and quilting bees, and its influence had extended to some 1,000 communities across the country.

One of the most newsworthy events in the evolution of the community-built movement was the planning and construction of an innovative playground in Ithaca, New York. A local architect, Robert S. Leathers, offered to help the school with the project and took a unique approach to it: he invited the students to be the prime planners of a "dream playground." He then rounded up the suggestions of parents, teachers, healthcare authorities, and civic leaders, and worked with them to organize a local army of volunteers. Like the worker bees of the pioneer barn raising, the volunteers then converged on the construction site and, within days, made the "dream playground" an exciting, lasting reality.

The Ithaca playground soon inspired the planning of similar projects in Rockport, Maine; Chestertown, Maryland; Orlando, Florida; and other communities. Most of those projects were initiated by parents, teachers, school administrators, park directors, and other local leaders with no previous experience in any of the building trades. When all the planning and organizing has been completed, the army of volunteers can usually build the playground, from start to finish, in about five days. The playground is designed to last at least 25 years.

For more information about the community-built playgrounds, write: Leathers & Associates, Inc., 99 Eastlake Road, Ithaca, NY 14850.

Homes for the Needy

Hurricane Andrew was Florida's worst storm in 60 years. When it ripped through the Miami area on August 24, 1992, with sustained winds of 140 mph, gusts up to 160 mph, and torrential rain, it turned old trailer parks into tangled wreckage and sheared the roofs off many of the most expensive homes and condominiums.

Amazingly, another category of home stood proudly intact after the storm, with little more than ruffled shingles to show for the ordeal.

The sturdy little survivors had been built by the volunteers of Habitat for Humanity.

In 1976, Habitat for Humanity was just another idea of Millard Fuller of Americus, Georgia, a man who had had lots of ideas, all focused on making money. At 29, he was "almost a millionaire." Then, suddenly, something inside him changed. He decided to give everything he owned away and start a new and different life with Habitat for Humanity. By 1988, Habitat for Humanity was being recognized by *Reader's Digest* and other major publications as an important national movement. By the time of Hurricane Andrew, in 1992, Habitat for Humanity had 800 affiliate organizations throughout the U.S. and the volunteer workers had built 18,000 homes.

Fuller had a conviction that everybody should have a decent home — but only if the person was willing to work for it. The work should be a helping hand — not a handout — and should be people-helping-people work, with no government involvement. He also thought of the concept as spiritual but not denominational; it would accept volunteers from any faith, and they would build homes for needy people of any faith.

Our friend Wanda Kohn is a fairly typical example of how a Habitat for Humanity affiliate comes into being. Wanda is in her mid-30s. She has worked as a licensed real estate broker, and she helps her husband, Bob, in his heating and air-conditioning business. She got involved in Habitat for Humanity after hearing Millard Fuller speak and has made it her full-time work ever since. She works, like the other volunteers, at no pay.

"We like retirees," Wanda tells us, "because they are so reliable — and because they are available to work during the week. Without retirees, it would be hard for Habitat for Humanity to continue its work."

The Needed Skills

Habitat for Humanity extends a special welcome to all retired members of the building trades: carpenters, masons, painters, electricians, roofers, and everybody else who can help train the other volunteers who will build the home—including the members of the family for whom the home is being built. The family for whom the home is being built must put at least 500 hours of "sweat equity" (labor) into the home, and must then assume a no-interest mortgage. Their monthly payments go into a fund for another mortgage for still another needy family.

"There is something very rewarding," says Wanda Kohn, "about building a home for somebody. One thing you learn is that the pride of home ownership can transform the people you help. They are no longer *renters* of what most of us would call *shacks*. Suddenly, they have a whole new kind of self-esteem, and a new sense of responsibility. And this feeling has a definite influence on their children, and on their neighbors. We now know that the children usually work for better grades in school, and the neighbors do a better job of keeping their places neater than before."

For more information, write to:

Habitat for Humanity International
121 Habitat St.
Americus, GA 31709-3498.

47

Getting Involved in Government

A nnette Andriola of San Diego developed a sudden and intense interest in politics long before she was old enough to vote. A family friend she trusted was also her town's boss of a political party. A few days before a local election, in which the principal voting would be for the mayor's post, the trusted friend told Annette, in solemn confidence, how he could destroy the chances of the honorable old incumbent with a last minute *"expose."*

The expose worked. It was based on a lie; but it effectively destroyed, at least temporarily, the lifetime reputation of the honorable old mayor. He never ran again.

"I never got over that cruel example of injustice," Annette told us later. "It still haunts me."

Later, she and her husband, Joseph, were invited to join the League of Women Voters to be better informed on all the issues. But that wasn't always enough. "The League often lost to some of the big, special-interest blocks. So I decided to get involved with one of the political parties."

In time, Annette was elected to an important county committee, then to an important state committee. "I didn't shape any great policies," she now concedes, "but I did have the opportunity to weed out some candidates I didn't trust. That was more satisfying than just voting in a primary election.

"Now I tell my grandchildren: democracy is a hard form of government to have. It takes a lot of work to keep it."

Your Vote Is Not Enough

Throughout recent times, citizens of retirement age have held all the records for best turnouts at the polls. When only 40-some percent of the youngest citizens were voting, an impressive 80-some percent of the seniors were exercising their right to choose the people who would lead them.

But even the senior leaders now admit: "It takes more than voting to make this country a better place. It takes becoming involved in the political process. How well do you know your representatives in city, county, state, and federal government? How well do you know their positions, their records — and where they got their campaign funds? To what extent did you actually participate in choosing those candidates?"

The League of Women Voters

One of the reasons why women like Annette Andriola take their right to vote so seriously is because it took women so long to win that right. Our American patriots declared the independence of their new democracy in 1776 — but it took the leaders of that democracy another 144 years before they stated, in 1920: "The right of citizens of the United States to vote shall not be denied or abridged by the United States or by any state on account of sex."

Amendment XIX gave women the right to vote and, in the same year, 1920, their leaders founded the League of Women Voters. Steadfastly, up through the years, the League of Women Voters has carried on the early New England town hall tradition of choosing political candidates on the basis of full public knowledge of who they are and what they stand for. The League describes itself as "political, not partisan; promoting issues, not candidates." The League monitors government at all levels, conducts and publishes impartial research, and promotes fair and open debates to inform the voters.

The League organized by women also wants to make it known that all *male* voters are also invited to join its ranks.

All Parties Need You

Some of the world's least-stable democracies have as many as 40 or even more political parties; we Americans have just two, and an occasional third. Their function is to set party rules, starting at the local level, and to select and support candidates for public office.

To have a personal influence on the shaping of local politics, you are invited to get in touch with the local executive committee of your favorite political party. Your county supervisor of elections can give you all the names you need.

Party organization begins with one or more committee persons in each voting precinct. Your county supervisor of elections will be glad to explain the local rules to you. Generally, to qualify to run for election to the post of precinct representative, all you need to be is an American citizen, a registered voter in that political party, and a resident of the precinct you are hoping to represent. Usually, there is no filing fee.

For more information about the League of Women Voters, just ask locally or write:

League of Women Voters of the United States
1730 M Street, NW
Washington, DC 20036

48

Wanted: Volunteers

No experience necessary, but must care about people

School needs aides in kindergarten and all grades.

Hospital needs women and men for variety of duties.

Chamber of Commerce needs greeters to guide tourists.

Homeless shelter needs help with child care.

Library needs all-around helpers.

Correctional institution needs tutors to help inmates work toward general education diploma.

Humane Society needs helpers at the pet shelter.

Hospice offers special training to volunteers to learn how to serve in patient and bereavement support.

Center for the Arts needs help in gift shop and gallery.

Preschoolers need help on vision and hearing screening.

Nursing Center needs musicians, craft leaders.

Adult literacy center needs tutors to teach English.

Meals-on-Wheels needs drivers. Mileage is paid.

Girl Scouts need leader for songs, games, crafts.

Cancer Society needs drivers to take patients to doctors' offices.

SCORE needs retired executives to serve as counselors to people who want to start their own business or need help in managing a small business.

Veterans group needs veteran for Honor Guard duties.

Adult day care center needs helper for music therapy, bingo.

Center for the blind needs volunteer to help train other volunteers.

Retarded citizens group needs gardening instructor.

Senior center needs help for its craft shop.

Museum of Art needs help in the gallery.

Food bank needs helpers.

Crisis hotline needs volunteers who like to be helpful to people who have problems.

Wildlife group needs help building shelters for orphaned wildlife.

Widowed outreach program will train counselors.

Red Cross needs volunteers for variety of duties.

Apply at RSVP

RSVP is the Retired Senior Volunteer Program, operated nationally by the federal government under the direction of *Action*, the National Volunteer Agency. RSVP acts as a clearing house for volunteers, working with scores of different public and non-profit organizations. RSVP performs the essential service of matching up the needs of the community with the personal interests of the volunteer.

Various surveys indicate that nearly 75 percent of all retirees are now volunteering in some way to help their families and their communities, and that about one-fourth of those retirees would be glad to donate even more time. The surveys also indicate that some 40 percent of all retirees believe the federal, state, and local governments should be doing more to promote volunteerism.

Why Volunteers Volunteer

People who direct volunteer programs report general gains in retiree interest in doing volunteer work. Part of the gain they attribute to wider awareness of global affairs, including the problems of the developing countries — "It all prods the people to take the world's problems more seriously, both abroad and at home."

Another part of the new interest in volunteerism, say the observers, is the highly predictable backlash against the self-centered "me" decade of the 1980s.

Still another force now winning compliments is the leadership of today's teen-agers: "The kids are setting some great examples for the older people to follow."

Historically, we are told, senior volunteers have favored activities associated with happiness — "making a child laugh"... "seeing a smile come to a shut-in's face."

And they liked to be helpful around hospitals — "but not close to death and dying."

Now, however, the observers are saying that basic attitudes toward serious troubles are changing in a significant way. They cite respite care as a good example.

Respite Care

Of all the kinds of care-giving, respite care is probably the kindness that is easiest for the giver to give, and most appreciated by the receiver.

"Respite," by dictionary definition, is simply "an interval of rest or relief." It gives some primary care giver a long-overdue "time out" for dinner with old friends, or a movie, or some shopping, or a morale-building trip to the hairdresser.

Respite care is usually associated with the adult day care facilities at Senior Centers and at many churches. But respite care is often at its thoughtful best when one caring person says to a home-bound care giver: "How about letting me do some sitting with your patient, some time this week, while you get out of the house for a while?"

In today's longer-living America, we are becoming acquainted with new health problems that didn't exist in earlier times, and often the problems are even more distressing to the primary care giver than they are to the patient. So a kindly offer to "do a little sitting" can sometimes be the greatest help any person can give another.

Helping the Helpers

One of our favorite workers in the volunteer world is Pastora Massad. She works for a church community with the responsibility of guiding its group of volunteers.

"Don't ever say *church*," she says, "when you mean church *commu-*

nity. A *church* is only a building; a *community* is people caring about other people."

Pastora follows a basic schedule: she and her volunteer group of 20-25 meet every three months and they go through the church membership cards. Each volunteer gets the names of 12 families in his or her own neighborhood. The volunteer, during the following week, will telephone the 12 families and make appointments for a personal visit. The visit will not include any mention of money for the church; it will be concerned only with any *problems* the family might be having. And then it will go one step further: the volunteer will ask if the family's *neighbors* are having any problems.

"We are trying to reach people who need help, but are too proud to ask for it," says Pastora. "We are trying to reach people who are *trying to help themselves.*

"We are not interested in the religion or color or nationality of any of these people. Our only question is: does this family, or this individual, need help?

"Sometimes they need food, and we have a pantry. Sometimes they are looking for work, and we know some people who can help. Sometimes they need money for rent, or for gasoline, and we don't have the money; but we can get in touch with the social agencies, and with other religious communities, and together we can make things come out all right.

"You ask me: do they always thank us? The answer is no. But you need to put yourself in their place on that. Many of them just don't know how to express gratitude. And many are ashamed to be asking for help — they have never had to do it before and, for many of them, this will be the *only* time.

"But there is one thing we notice that is very important.

"The people we help will tend later to *help other people.* It's exciting to watch this happen."

Pastora's phone is ringing again. She picks up the receiver and cups her hand over the mouthpiece. "But the really *big* point," she says, "is what this work is doing for our volunteers. They feel needed again; they feel more involved in what's going on in the world. So tell your friends to come see us — we can use more help for these helpers."

Helping the World

On March 1, 1961, President John F. Kennedy announced the formation of a U.S. Peace Corps to aid developing countries. The report continued: "Kennedy envisions volunteers, mostly youths just out of college, going to less advantaged countries and teaching secondary school, assisting in health education, or advising on agricultural matters."

By the 1990s, one in every 12 Peace Corps volunteers was over the age of 50, and many were in their 80s. One reason for the graying of the Corps is that it learned to place high value on the unique experience of the older volunteers. A second reason is that the Peace Corps works in countries where age is greatly respected. The basic facts are these:

Eligibility. Applicants must be U.S. citizens and at least 18 years old. There is no upper age limit. Married couples are eligible if both can work. All applicants must be medically qualified. Some programs require professional degrees.

Service. The normal tour of service is 24 months, following three months of training. All volunteers receive language and cultural training, usually in the country where they will be serving. Strong emphasis is placed on learning the host country language. Cultural studies include the history, customs, and the social and political systems of the host country.

Skills needed. Peace Corps volunteers work in a variety of self-help development programs: rural health, family nutrition, fresh water fisheries, agriculture extension, teacher training, math and science education, vocational training, small business consulting, natural resource development, forestry, conservation, and energy.

Countries served. The Peace Corps now serves 65 nations in Latin America, Africa, Asia, and the Pacific. Volunteers may express their geographic preference.

Benefits. While in training and during service, the volunteer receives a monthly allowance for rent, food, travel, and all medical needs. Transportation is provided to training sites, and to and from the overseas assignment, as well as for home leave in the event of family emergencies. A readjustment allowance is set aside, payable upon successful completion of service. All volunteers are covered by Federal Employees Compensation in case of disabilities incurred during their tour, and a life insurance policy is offered as an option.

For more information, call 1-800-424-8580 (toll free), or write, with information about yourself, to: Peace Corps of the United States, Box 941, Washington, DC 20526.

49

TV: Your Window
on the World

At first the progress was slow; then it was breathless.

In January 1926, a Scottish inventor named John L. Baird showed London's Royal Institution a new machine he called "television." Two years later, Baird made the first overseas television broadcast, London to New York.

In April 1939, David Sarnoff of RCA became the "father of American television" by introducing the first U.S. television receiver at the New York World's Fair. He told his audience very earnestly: "This is a creative force which we must learn to utilize for the benefit of all mankind. ... *It is the use to which the new invention is put, and not the invention itself, that determines its value to society.*"

One year later, President Franklin D. Roosevelt announced that the Federal Communications Commission (FCC) would develop rules to prevent any group from monopolizing the new medium of commercial television, which was expected to start in the fall.

Commercial television, supported by advertisers, was soon on its way to giving us a front-row seat at all the best comedy, musicals, sporting events, and news happenings. Television, within a decade, was a national phenomenon.

But there were indications, by the end of that first decade, that television was not living up to the hopes of David Sarnoff.

A 1950 study showed that children were spending as much time (27 hours a week) watching TV as they spent in school and that homework was suffering. A year later, the *New York Times* reported that television had already changed American society more than any force since the coming of the automobile, and that television was exerting a major influence on how we spend our leisure time, how much we read, how we feel about politics, and "even on the way we rear our children."

Also in 1950, the Ford Foundation began a major study of how the culture level of television could be raised.

Ratings vs. Quality

To find out how much they should charge advertisers, television networks needed to know how many people, and of what ages, were watching the various programs. Various rating methods were tried. By 1950, inventor A.C. Nielsen's "Audimeter" — installed in a little more than 1,000 homes — was reporting numbers and generating "ratings" that would help decide the programming for all the other homes in America.

By the 1990s, the Nielsen research sample had grown to about 4,000 — which meant that the viewing habits of each Nielsen home would set the quality standards for the programs to be seen more than 23,000 other TV homes.

And how was the standard-setting Nielsen householder selected? Education? Demonstrated good judgment? No — the Nielsen householder could be described simply as "a randomly selected demographic statistic."

By the 1990s, television had beamed so much violence and sex and obscenity across the nation that one FCC Commissioner, James H. Quello, observed wryly, "Instead of having *prime*-time television serving the *public* interest, we now have *slime*-time television serving the *pubic* interest."

Unfortunately for Quello, the homes in the Nielsen sample continued to tune in to violence, sex, and obscenity. Quello, a former broadcaster, continued to argue: "The broadcasters want the cost-per-thousand and the demographics; but we need a goal that's higher than cost-per-thousand and demographics."

With Commissioner Quello leading the charge, the FCC moved against broadcasting stations that were violating FCC rules governing indecency and obscenity and levied fines totalling more than $700,000 on stations in four major cities. Quello concluded: "Everybody in a station has a First Amendment right to be outrageous and stir people up — but nobody has a First Amendment right to violate our indecency rules. And it isn't just the individual performer who's going to get nailed — it's going to be the licensee, because nobody can abdicate licensee responsibility."

The Coming of Cable

Cable TV moved slowly into the scene in the early 1960s, serving hilly areas where home antennas couldn't deliver a clear picture, and took 20 years to account for 25% of TV homes.

By then, television advertisers were aware that cable TV offered a whole new variety of highly select markets. Now, in the 1990s, cable TV serves about two-thirds of all TV homes. The three giant networks, which had nearly 90 percent of TV homes as their viewers in the early 1960s, had dropped to less than 60 percent of all TV homes by the early 1990s.

A typical TV home now has a choice not just of several important channels with similar shows but of 50 or more channels, many with the very finest educational and cultural standards. No longer is a tiny "demographic statistic" holding everybody else hostage. To make their viewing even more selective, more and more families now pick and choose the very best offerings of all the channels with video cassette recorders (VCRs).

What's Coming Next?

The 1990s are now seeing a rush of new technologies: direct broadcast satellites in the cable TV industry, fiber optics in the television industry — plus high-definition television. The cable TV industry, the telephone industry, and the information services industry are competing for leadership in moving onto what some observers call "the coming worldwide electronic highway." Our own area is about to receive the world's first mega-cable TV system that carries interactive video, telephone, and informational services. It would transform our TV remote control unit into a portable wireless phone, a computer keyboard, and a changer for hundreds of video channels. We will be able to talk to our TV, and the TV will talk back.

FCC Commissioner James H. Quello, a Democrat appointed by President Nixon in 1974 and reappointed by three subsequent presidents, has been through all the battles to become the dean of the FCC. Opposed originally by consumer groups because he was a broadcaster, he came to be known as "the champion of the public interest model for regulating broadcasting." He also served as a front-line infantry battalion commander in World War II and is a rock-jawed individual who votes his conscience and has never been pushed around by special interest groups. So we wrote to Commissioner Quello and asked him if he would give our readers a forecast of what's ahead in TV. He did. It follows.

The Quello View

"It is now 1993. For at least the next five years, I believe the FCC's highest priority will be the orderly, compatible implementation of the advanced technologies of high definition television (HDTV), fiber optics, telecomputing, digital audio broadcasting (DAB), cellular, and personal communications services.

"I visualize a future with cable and phone companies as major multi-channel and phone competitors with Congress requiring guarantees of free or favored access for stations licensed to serve the public interest.

"The rate and extent of technological development will be controlled by consumer acceptance and affordability, commercial practicalities, legislative and regulatory actions, and —ultimately — by the way the service benefits the public interest.

"The bedrock of my own regulatory philosophy is, and always has been, the preservation and expansion of universal free broadcast service for all Americans."

50

Newspapers: Keeping You Up With the Times

Pittsburgh, in recent times, experienced a strike that deprived it of its newspapers. The people took it calmly at first: it was simple enough to just switch on the TV or radio to get the news,

But then came a growing, uneasy feeling throughout the community, that something very important was¡ missing.

Job hunters, without Help Wanted ads, were in despair.

Stores remained almost empty during critical sales.

Vacant houses and apartments had few or no takers.

Even funeral directors began to complain. Said one: "We're getting frantic calls from friends of the family that they didn't know when the services would be held."

The Need to Know

Newspapers are so reliable, so taken-for-granted, that we sometimes don't appreciate them until the presses go silent. Our need to know can become a distressing mental hunger.

Lee Stinnett, Executive Director of the American Society of Newspaper Editors, tells us: "Reading papers helps retirees find ways to participate fully in community life. Newspaper reading is educational, stimulating, sometimes aggravating — with plenty to keep the mind active. Newspaper reading is something you can do at your own easy pace, whenever you feel like doing it. Also, newspapers are inexpensive — and many newspapers have increased body type sizes to accommodate older readers who may have trouble with smaller type."

Here are some of the specials on the daily buffet menu of most newspapers:

- An update, in depth, on what's going on in your community, your state, your country, and the rest of the world. It's in print, so you can read it at your leisure, clip and save it, and share it with your near and faraway friends. The news includes announcements of births, weddings, personal triumphs and failures, deaths, and all the scores of the local high school teams on which somebody's grandchildren play. The news also includes a calendar of local events in which retirees enjoy participating.

• Cultural guidance on the best in books and theater, folk and art festivals, museums, music and travel.

• Business guidance on all the major industries as well as the local scene — plus the most up-to-date report on the stock markets.

• Civic and political guidance from editorials and from advice columns that keep us aware of all sides of the issues. Still other columns keep us informed about emotional and medical hazards and how to deal with them.

• Marketplace guidance from the ads about the best values in foods, clothing, and almost everything else.

• And don't forget the comics. Ever since "The Yellow Kid" and "The Katzenjammer Kids" of 1897, the comics have been one of the best-read parts of any paper. The comics have encouraged youngsters to read and oldsters to laugh.

Newspapers Are Local

When Cliff and Donita Paine were editing and publishing their *Fennville Herald,* they never knew, from week to week, how they would collect enough news to put out a paper. They referred to theirs as "the weekly gamble." But the people of Fennville always counted on the *Herald* to be there with whatever news there was. And they often counted on its editorials to serve as "the conscience of the community."

"Without a newspaper," one Fennville reader once told us, "a person could be born, live, and die without a lot of people knowing he had even *been* here."

51

Keeping in Touch

When Joyce D. Hall of Kansas City invented the modern greeting card, in 1916, he based it on a very simple hunch: *most people lack either the words or the confidence to express their sentimental feelings to anyone else.* He put his hunch to an early test with a card that simply stated: "Just to let you know that I'm thinking of you."

The wistfully sentimental little greeting card was soon on its way to accounting for half of all U.S. personal mail, and Joyce D. Hall of Hallmark was credited with being the father of the booming new "Social Expression Industry."

Browsing through the everywhere-displays of greeting cards for all occasions is still the most popular way to say, "I'm thinking of you." But today's retirees keep inventing other fresh approaches as rivals to the cards. Here's a sampling:

- New recipes. If it tasted good to you, share it with a friend. The photocopying machines make it easy to multiply your favorite, along with a personal note.

- Photographs. Always good. A thoughtful way to share your day with someone who can't be with you. The best pictures, of course, are the growing-up keepsakes of the grandchildren — they always disappear before we know it into adulthood. You can encourage more of this living history with a gift camera to the parents.

- Clippings. The newspapers are a daily gold mine: cartoons for laughs. Stories, or even just mentions, of your friend, or of something of special interest to him or her. Quaint facts he or she would enjoy as much as you did.

- New products. Anything you bought and liked enough to recommend it to a friend. Just a box top, or a cutout from an ad, with a simple note.

- Audio tapes. Music from anywhere. Conversations with mutual friends. Some messages that are easier to say than to spell out on paper.

- Video tapes. Documentaries of special interest to an old friend who probably missed them when they first ran. Musicals you thought were delightful and wanted to share. Dramas not everybody had a chance to see.

And Letters

Especially in the retirement years, everybody hopes for a letter in the day's mail — so why don't more people write letters? Sometimes it's because nobody has written them a letter they need to answer. So be the first and see what you get in return.

One of our favorite letter writers is Thorn Kuhl, ex-wire service reporter, who retired in Hackettstown, New Jersey, and took Mary and their golf clubs to Carrboro, North Carolina.

For the past 25 years, in addition to his duties as a public relations executive, Thorn has been writing newsletters for his college in Iowa, keeping up a correspondence with 125 or more classmates. So we asked Thorn to give our readers some tips on the writing of letters. Here are his suggestions:

"If I had to boil it down to just a few points," Thorn writes, "I'd settle for these:

"**One:** when I sit down to write a letter, I just pretend that the person I'm writing to is sitting across the desk from me. I just write as if I were talking to that person.

"**Two:** I always try to write the kind of letter I would like to receive. Bits of news about family and mutual friends; some special comments about Mary's volunteer work at the hospital; perhaps a few opinions about what's happening in our town and state. Nothing boastful, sad, or controversial. I don't have a right to involve my faraway friends in any of my personal problems or dislikes.

"**Three:** before I start writing, I reflect for a few moments on what I would like to know about them, and then write accordingly. A good letter, I think, should show a real interest in the receiver and the receiver's life and activities.

"Friends tell me," he concludes, "that I should have a memory typewriter on which I could program a number of different paragraphs, so that I could use them as inserts in my letter. I might get to that if somebody can pry me away from this 1953 Royal manual typewriter."

Being There

There's no substitute, of course, for your personal presence. You can share it daily by just sharing your time at restaurants, movies, county fairs, concerts, and all the other happy occasions with someone who might otherwise be "left out."

And you can plan vacation trips that include visits with people who are very dear to you. They won't be there forever.

Finally, there's the *phone* — the next-best thing to being there in person. And the phone works two ways: you can call them, and they can call you. Sometimes, the best kind of friendship you can offer is just to *be* there, always ready to listen and to understand.

Index

About the Authors

David and Virginia Cleary, who retired early, have been widely and deeply involved in the retirement world for 25 years. They have served in their state's Silver-Haired Legislature, concerned with senior affairs at the state level, and on the board of their county Council on Aging, running a senior services center. They also have worked as volunteers in their local mental health center, and as volunteers in Southeast Asia for the International Executive Service Corps, handling marketing and teaching assignments.

Before retirement, David was a V.P. and partner in Young & Rubicam, a major international advertising agency with headquarters in New York City. He directed the creative work on such accounts as American Airlines, Goodyear tires, and Lincoln cars. Much earlier, during World War II, he served as a front-line commander in a First Army spearhead across Germany.

Virginia Glynn Cleary was accepted as a graduate exchange student at the University of St. Andrews in Scotland under the first Fulbright Scholarship program. She later served with the U.S. Foreign Service in Athens, Greece, administering Marshall Plan funds. Back in the U.S., she managed food and banquet services at the airline executives' Wings Club in New York City. Still later, she moved south and worked as a commercial loan administrator in a major bank.

Both were widowed in retirement. After their marriage, they launched a local opinion and marketing research service in Tampa that soon brought orders for national surveys, and they continue to be active as marketing consultants.

They also collaborated on a marketing casebook, *Great American Brands*: the success formulas that made them famous, which was exhibited nationally by the American Library Association as part of its collection of "Outstanding Books of the Year."

After sharing the parenting of four highly active and individualistic children, they are now enjoying the carefree role of being grandparents to another fascinating four.

Over time, David and Virginia Cleary have had close-up experience with nearly all the joys and problems and anxieties of retirement living. Now they tell us: "We have learned to take it one day at a time, always remembering that today is all we have, and that we need some bad days to help us appreciate the good ones."

ALLWORTH BOOKS